CITIES MATTER

CITIES MATTER

A Montrealer's Ode

to

JANE JACOBS,
Economist

Charles-Albert Ramsay

Baraka Books

Montréal

ISBN 978-1-77186-304-9 pbk; 978-1-77186-310-0 epub; 978-1-77186-311-7 pdf

Cover by Folio infographie
Book Design by Folio infographie
Editing and proofreading: Robin Philpot, Daniel J. Rowe, Blossom Thom

Legal Deposit, 4th quarter 2022
Bibliothèque et Archives nationales du Québec
Library and Archives Canada

Published by Baraka Books of Montreal

Printed and bound in Quebec

Trade Distribution & Returns
Canada – UTP Distribution: UTPdistribution.com

United States
Independent Publishers Group: IPGbook.com

We acknowledge the support from the Société de développe-ment des entreprises culturelles (SODEC) and the Government of Quebec tax credit for book publishing administered by SODEC.

Société
de développement
des entreprises
culturelles
Québec

Funded by the Government of Canada
Financé par le gouvernement du Canada | Canada

Contents

Foreword

People ask themselves why cities exist? Can't there be other ways of organizing life on earth? Given the climate crisis and environmental concerns, how can we justify building taller buildings, and living in cramped quarters?

This book will answer those questions. There are really good reasons why cities exist. There are also really good reasons to believe that cities can help us solve the problems of our day and age.

The book's main value proposition is to corral much of the economic theory in Jane Jacobs' writing, in a palatable and concise format. The book also explains classical economic geography theory, such as central location theory, and Alfred Marshall's economies of agglomeration. The book proposes real-life exercises for regular people who wish to compare suburban and urban living conditions, real estate investments, as well as transport-cost analysis in a business case.

I would like to thank the following colleagues and professors for their help in sharing their ideas and insights about cities and the economy. Dr. Petr Hanel, Dr. Richard Shearmur, Dr. Roma Dauphin, Dr. Jean-Philippe Meloche, James Roberts, Sacha Des Rosiers, and Dr. Worku Aberra.

Introduction

Why do cities exist? I've been asking myself that question for a long time. I really like cities. I like walking through them, biking around in them, and hanging out in their restaurants. A lot of people take the fact of cities for granted, "that's just the way things are, right?"

Well, there IS a reason for cities. And the main reason is the economic reason. This is the whole point of this book. The economics of cities are driving all sorts of other phenomena.

If you look at it from other angles, you will find that cities have a lot of explaining to do! Politically, cities are a little problematic. They grow taller and wider and generate lots of tension between rural areas and urban ones. Socially, they have their pros and cons, the first mostly being the possibility of a cosmopolitan lifestyle, where you can eat exotic meals, see cutting-edge art, and meet people from all over the world. The latter being the insecurity, traffic, pollution, and general anguish that cities can generate. Historically, cities have not existed as long as humans. So technically we don't need cities to exist as a species on planet earth. Geographically, cities often grow in areas where resources are really scarce, or where there is barely even any land. Environmentally speaking, cities seem to encourage the over-consumption of resources and constantly create new types of pollution.

Given our recent past with pandemics and all, you might be wondering, are cities doomed? Are people going to work from home all the time and leave the downtown office towers? This question has been on many people's minds, including landowners, real estate investors, regular families, and policy makers.

You might be asking yourself, should I buy a house in the city? In the suburbs? In a small town? Help!!!

My answer to all of this is NO, cities are not doomed.

Does that mean you should buy a house in the core? That's not for me to say. Although I love strategizing other people's lives, especially my friends' lives, this book is not about advice. Don't call me and complain about how you bought a condo and hate it.

Back to our main point: this book is about the economics that explains the glue that binds people together in tight, awkward spaces. Hopefully, you will agree, cities still have a role to play in saving our human civilization. And also, hopefully, you will come to appreciate the epic wisdom of one smart lady: Jane Jacobs.

Jane Jacobs is an American author (she moved to Toronto in the late sixties) who is responsible for changing the way we think about cities, especially about urban planning. When you see cities all over the world tearing down highways, and rebuilding old-style walkable neighbourhoods, they are using the Jacobs playbook. If you hear economists lauding the innovation and diversity of metropolitan economies, they are applying and repeating the principles that Jacobs laid out in her books.

Her first book came out in 1959, *The Death and Life of Great American Cities*. It was a harsh criticism of New York City's urban planning since the end of World War II. She had gained most of her insights from walking the city's neighborhoods, on assignment for *The New York Times* newspaper. She would notice that some neighborhoods seemed to be safer, and livelier, than others. She also noticed that this was not due to higher incomes, but rather to the physical infrastructure, the street layouts, the shape and density of housing, the availability of commercial rentals on the street levels, and the way automobiles were dominating, or not, the landscape. In many cases, the worst living conditions were found in the newer housing projects, which had cost taxpayers millions of dollars. Being married to an architect, she discussed these issues at home, but also at the newspaper, and with readers. A brilliant self-taught learner, she spent hours in libraries reading about classical urban planning, and the sociology of cities.

Jacobs then put much thought into the next logical aspect of city life, its economy. In her 1969 book *The Economy of Cities*, she reframed classical economic modelling around the geography of the city, rather than the political nation. By doing so, she re-imagined the trade cycles of cities, and how that leads to product innovation, business opportunity, and city growth.

Reading these principles of economic life, while I was a younger university student, changed my mind about economics. At the time, in the early aughts, her theories were not part of the curriculum, even if her books were decades old. I felt a little bit like a *mouton noir*, as an undergraduate in an economics department where most professors, and students, were more interested in monetary theory, public finance, labour markets, and advanced statistical analysis. I have to thank Dr. Petr Hanel, my master's thesis director at Université de Sherbrooke, for accepting my proposal and allowing me to test one of Jacobs' hypotheses using patent data. The data confirmed the Jacobs hypothesis that large cities are associated with product innovation, while outside areas focus on new cost-cutting processes.

Jacobs' economic theory is more akin to an older tradition called political economy, while not necessarily being left-wing. Her work does not sit well with complex mathematical modelling. Many readers see parallels in Jacobs' work with the Austrian school of economic thought, which shares her focus on productive investment, entrepreneurship, and a literal understanding of production methods. One detail I really like about Jacobs is that she insists on listing products that are produced in a certain economy, instead of using broad industrial categories. For me, this shows that she cares about the reality of production—an on-the-ground empirical preoccupation that feels more like fieldwork, than anonymous statistical analysis.

Hopefully, learning about Jane Jacobs will help you, as it helped me, to understand the urban world we live in, and hopefully, you will feel more empowered to make that decision on where to live.

Why so much economics about cities? Well, first, I'm an economist. Second, cities ARE the economy. If you, like me, prefer to learn in the field than in front of an Excel spreadsheet, then look around and what do you see? The city is the labour market. The city is the produce market. The city is the international market. The city IS the market. Even with the internet, the city is evermore the market, the economy.

I am not saying that there is no economy outside the city, rather that that economy is defined by the city.

You may ask: "Why should I care? I don't care about the economy."

Ok, fine. But why are global populations urbanizing, and fast? Did you know that this is affecting everything from your job to income disparities, to trade routes, and yes, you guessed it, to pandemics?

For a long time, economists have neglected the historic and central role of cities in economic growth and prosperity. Cities are economies. They organize production and create opportunities for new markets. Cities have funded the most ambitious emperors, and then, when the cities were no longer dynamically creating new production, the empires fell.

As you are going to learn in this book, cities don't always function properly. Healthy cities make for prosperous countries and unhealthy cities have dangerous consequences. So not only is it fascinating, but it's really important, too.

This book is intended for curious minds who are looking for a window into a new world of intellectual curiosity, which is precisely what Jacobs did for me, when I was 20 years old.

SECTION 1

The Economist's City

In this section, we are going to discuss what classical economists can explain about cities. It's really quite useful. Economists are good at thinking in terms of costs of production, including transportation costs, so that's actually a really big deal. Economists are also good at analyzing markets, using supply and demand theory. That's a really important tool if you want to make an investment in real estate.

CHAPTER 1

Economies of Agglomeration

Why would a company want to locate near one of its competitors? There would have to be a strong argument to convince the owners that moving into a cluster of similar producers would bring some kind of benefit to the bottom line.

For some companies, being in a city is just not worth it. That is a fact. They would much prefer to be located in an isolated area where they could control almost every aspect of the production line. There are many cases like this, such as the old Kodak industrial complex in Rochester, New York, or the Bombardier snowmobile facilities located in Valcourt, Quebec.

For other companies, it's important to be in a relatively large city, but they don't necessarily want to be neighbors with their competition. Think of Boeing, whose location in Seattle, Washington, is quite far from other airplane producers elsewhere in the US, Canada, France, Germany, Britain, China, Brazil, and elsewhere.

But for many other companies and organizations, if not most of them, there are great benefits to being in a large, vibrant, diverse city, even if your competitors are just next door. Those benefits have to do with cost savings that small companies can tap into, even if they are too small to benefit from traditional economies of scale. These are called economies of agglomeration.

More than 100 years ago, a British economist named Alfred Marshall (1920) proposed three reasons why producers can save money when locating their factories near other companies. He was trying to understand why there was such a cluster of industrial activity in the working districts of London, Manchester, Birmingham, and other English cities.

He started talking about an agglomeration as being a cluster of factories, stores, and other businesses. There was nothing new to this, cities have been around for a long time. But he was putting his finger on the precise economic reasons why clustering helps your business.

By the way, Marshall was a prolific writer and an important economist. He wrote about all sorts of economic topics. He wrote the first formal economics university manual. He taught his theory of supply and demand to none other than the famous John Maynard Keynes.

Marshall argued that agglomerations help each company save money and improve their efficiency. These economies of cost are due to the location of the company in a city, which is a synonym for agglomeration. Marshall's theory of "Economies of Agglomeration" is still used today to explain why cities exist.

Let's start with the basics. If a company does not cluster with other producers, it would be located in a rural area, such as a rather small town. The only way to reduce costs is to grow the company. By increasing your sales, you can increase the specialization of each worker, increase the use of machines, and each unit becomes less expensive to produce. This is a well-known concept called "economies of scale."

For example, if you make chairs in a small workshop, your workers will each have to accomplish several distinct operations in the same day. In a large-scale factory, each worker specializes on one step, which makes everything go faster and become more efficient. This improvement in productivity reduces the average cost of production. We could say the cost improvements are done inside the company, or internally.

Most people think that you can't achieve these economies without scale. Sounds reasonable.

Well, Marshall proposes that small workshops can become just as efficient as large factories, while still staying small. But this can only be done in the city, where small workshops have access to highly specialized inputs. We could say these cost improvements happen outside the workshop, through specialized suppliers, or externally.

In short, "economies of agglomeration" are another way of saying "external economies of scale."

The three Economies of Agglomeration are

A) Shared pool of labour
B) Input sharing
C) Knowledge spillovers

The first economy has to do with the lower cost of acquiring labour in the city, where companies can "share" labour. For example, aerospace companies would benefit from being in Seattle, or in Montreal because these cities already hire many specialists in this field. The city will probably train more people in this field, so it will be possible to hire young recruits, or even poach some older workers from competitors.

Second, producers would benefit from a larger market for raw materials. Since Montreal produces airplanes, it is easy to find inputs such as aluminum and specialized electronics in Montreal. This attracts even more aerospace companies. Cities often offer a hub of transportation networks, ports, airports, highways, which reduce the transportation costs of inputs and outputs.

Third, producers can learn from one another in the city. Some companies really do not want this, as their need for secrecy is important. They are the ones who would rather isolate themselves. Most companies would probably believe that they would benefit from isolation. However, knowledge spillovers are usually good for the system as a whole, which means they would be good for each of the companies as well.

The knowledge spills over from one producer to the next, and especially potently across industries. This happens in many ways. If a worker is laid off, they may find work elsewhere. The competition now has access to technical or market information of great value. Some companies go out of their way to poach the most productive employees, but mostly those who have the most information to bridge over. Another form of spillover is to hire part-time consultants and specialists, such as technical experts or university scientists. Their work in the university lab then spills over to the private sector. Other forms of spillage include specialized local media, word-of-mouth, industry associations, and networking events.

Cities have taken this ball and ran with it. Today, most people on earth live in large cities. Economies are wealthier and more urban than ever. Urban economies are also more innovative. In Quebec, 76[1] percent of patent activity was performed in the Greater Montreal area, which only represents half of Quebec's population.

What can non-urban economies do? It seems they have had to focus on offering low-cost inputs such as labour, or natural resources. When so endowed, think of potash in Saskatchewan, or cheap labour in China, these areas can prosper. However, their lack of diversity will leave these economies vulnerable to foreign demand shocks. We will talk about this in more detail later in the book.

Problems Created by Cities

Sure, companies can save money if they locate together. But what about traffic? When is the last time you were stuck in a congested highway turnpike, Ramsay?

Touché. You make a good point. I hate traffic just like anybody else. The problem with cities is the problems they create. At first, it's all fun and games, but then it gets complicated as the density of the city grows, until it maxes out the infrastructure.

It's true, cities create many problems. Successful cities grow sometimes uncontrollably, creating havoc for their citizens. Traffic, pollution, and crime are just some of the problems that can become unbearable in large cities.

As I try to imagine what the first city-induced issues might have been, I can imagine scarcity of food, and energy to cook. Even about 100 years ago, Montrealers were heating their homes with wood and coal in the winter. Those large pine trees on the Island that Samuel de Champlain wrote about, they are long gone. They were cut down and were used to make carts, homes, boats, and firewood. This city could probably never be able to produce all the food that Montrealers need to eat and thrive. Once all the wood on the island has been cut to build houses, where will the energy come from to heat them for the next decades and centuries?

So, cities are just doomed? I knew it!

No. The magic is right here. Healthy cities find solutions to their problems. People are hungry? Let's import food from surrounding areas, and turn the land into farms. People need fuel for their ovens? Let's invent new energy sources, and new kinds of furnaces and ovens.

Healthy cities are likely to be creative, find solutions, or outright invent solutions to deal with their problems. Cities have invented things like

- Corn, a more productive food plant.
- Tractors, a more productive earth-moving technology.
- Sewers and Aqueducts, more effective water management.
- Electricity, a cleaner and more convenient energy source.
- Cars, Trains, Planes: faster, cleaner, and more productive than horse and buggy.

Many authors such as Jacobs (1969) argue that a city's ability to invent, and innovate, and solve urban problems is the key to constant economic development and growth.

What helps a city solve problems?

There is no one definitive answer to this question. It is very difficult to pinpoint the exact cause-and-effect relationships that lead to diverse and inventive cities. The answers that Jacobs proposes are very interesting. The cities that are growing and dynamic are now dubbed Jacobs' agglomerations by contemporary academics. Jacobs believed cities should try to master all the elements of the urban ecology, which are:

Good markets, the right kind of urban planning, strong science, a propensity to reinvest profits, a propensity to invest productively, a diverse industrial base, a healthy labour force, openness to new ideas, and the ability to reverse-engineer and locally produce key imports.

Cities can constantly create new problems, which can be salutary in the sense that these problems create opportunities to generate new solutions. These new solutions can spur new industries and fuel economic development and growth.

However, cities can become vulnerable to these problems and fail. Many, many, cities have fallen in history due to inadequate economic growth and crushing social problems such as pollution and crime. Hence, we should look at city problems as opportunities to innovate, and find new solutions. Strategies for economic development can thus actually be inspired by our love-hate relationship with cities.

What do you really love about cities? When you travel, you can discover all sorts of products, services, and ideas, that you can bring back home and use as fodder for a business opportunity, to solve a social issue, or to simply make your neighbourhood more fun to live in.

What do you really hate about cities? When you move around your city, you will notice lots of problems. Sometimes it feels overwhelming. However, if you tackle a city problem, you are most likely to create economic opportunity out of it. It's not a question of focussing on greed, or profit-seeking, it has more to do with improving the well being of your family and community. When Paris decided to tackle the lack of sanitation and water pollution in the poorer *arrondissements,* the outer rings boroughs, the city was forced to invest in much research and development to invent modern-day plumbing and aqueducts. Today, French water engineers are sought out everywhere on the planet for their expertise. A solution to a social problem often leads to economic development.

When most people I know think about cities, especially young people, they usually think about museums, night clubs and restaurants, and they usually don't have much to say about the negatives, except for a little bit of traffic. I've come to believe that a city without problems might actually be a little bit problematic!

CHAPTER 2

Hub Cities and Transport Costs

It's hard to model diverse, complex systems. In economics, we tend to think in terms of straight lines, and hard logic. This does not work so well in living settings, where networks are more important than linear relationships. And that's what a city is. It is a living, breathing, changing, and developing network of relationships.

This is precisely why the land in the city is worth so much money. When your system is a set of networks, being in the middle of the action can pay off.

Sounds pretty philosophical. Well, there is also a very logical way to look at it. If you have to manage a project, or a business, you are going to have to think of things coming together. Sometimes you need those things to actually come together physically. The geography matters. Things that move slowly cost more money to bring in. Things that move longer distances also cost more. If you can choose a location where you could reduce most of your transportation costs, that would make sense to you, and your accountant.

This is where the hub comes into play.

Cities are usually transportation hubs. Places where boats and trucks meet planes and trains, and any other mode of transportation. Producers who locate in these hubs reduce transportation costs, as long as congestion is not too important. The hub effect is so strong, that sometimes if you build a hub, a city will grow out of 'nowhere'.

Jane Jacobs (1969) argued that cities, being where the consumer market is, are natural locations for producers. However, cities can become congested, which seems inefficient. It is terribly inefficient. Having your product stuck in traffic, does not make for a happy camper. If the city does not tend to its problems of congestion, producers will leave to lower-density locations where land is cheap, and traffic is naught.

Jacobs understood the problem, but she argued the issue was more complex than this. She argues that cities also reduce the transport costs of inputs to production. Producers can leave the city because of traffic, but where are they going to get their materials? They need to be close to the inputs, or at least need to be able to reduce their input transportation costs.

The problem for businesspeople is that inputs are usually diverse and may need to be imported from a variety of locations. Being centrally located, and endowed with transportation hubs, cities reduce the overall transportation cost of gathering these inputs. (See diagram 1.)

So even if cities become somewhat congested, their central location keeps companies around, especially if they have to source their inputs from diverse locations. The key to understanding what this means is to consider the diversity and variety of inputs that go into the production of even simple products.

To explain this, geographers and economists use a simple model called the 'Input Location— Transport Cost' theory. You can find this in any first-year economic geography university manual. The model simplifies the producer's situation to having four inputs, and one output. The four inputs can be natural resources like wood, or transformed materials like leather. Imagine a flat land with no obstacles, no mountains, no rivers, and no lakes. The four inputs each have their region, which are equally spaced out apart. Imagine roads that link each region to its neighbor, but there are no roads that go across through the middle of the land.

Let's say the company is making an office chair, using wood from the North, plastic wheels from the South, foam from the West, and leather from the East.

The company has to choose a location where to make the chairs. I would pick the wooded area because that's heavy to transport, and makes up a big part of a chair. This would be the simplest way to reduce my transportation costs. I would need plastic

DIAGRAM 1
Input Location – Transport Cost Model – Equidistant
locations

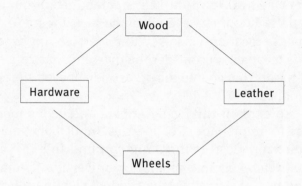

wheels to be trucked from the South. Another truck
would pick up foam in the West. A third would bring
leather from the East. If we keep this simple, I've got
four units of road transport to pay for.

So now you ask, when are you going to start
talking about the hub?

Let's say the government has money to spend on
new roads. They build two roads, each going across
from North to South, and East to West. Each of these
roads is longer than the previous roads. Assuming
a square angle where these roads cross, we've got a
pretty powerful model.

Because now the lowest cost location is the middle location.

But wait, I still need four truck trips because I no
longer produce in the woodlands.

True, but each of those trips is shorter.

Remember your 7th grade math class when you asked your teacher, "When am I ever going to use the Pythagorean theorem?"

Well, now. Pythagoras is the glue that holds cities together. Think about that!

If you check the math, it's true. The roads going to the middle are shorter than the roads on the outside. The hub linking those regions will naturally be chosen as the manufacturing and assembly site, as it reduces the overall transportation costs of the inputs. Assuming the transport costs are equivalent (weights, volumes, etc.) between the inputs, the cheapest production location is E.

What's neat about the model is that you can increase the number of inputs, and the hub always wins.

You may object that companies must also consider the transportation costs of the final good to the market. Somebody has to buy the product.

Good point, at first there is no market in the middle, it's empty. But as production moves there, so do workers, and hence, demand follows supply.

CHAPTER 3

Urban Land Values

Why are land prices so high in the middle of cities?

City properties tend to be very expensive. The most dynamic cities are famous for driving up housing prices. If you own land in the city, you will benefit from this. If you rent, then maybe you won't.

An important nuance on this topic is that houses don't increase in value. Only land increases in value. But the market is mostly for built-up plots of land, where most of the time, buyers will live in the house that's already there. So, buyers are buying a house. You can't really live on land, if there isn't a house on it. This creates a distortion in people's minds about what is growing in value.

Houses are constantly in need of upkeep and repair. They depreciate, just like most physical assets. So, it makes no sense to believe that they increase in value. How can a house, that needs $100,000 in renovations, be worth more than when it was built? The answer is in the land.

If you shop for homes in isolated rural areas, you can buy a lot of home for your money. This is because the land has less value. The same house in the city can be worth five times the money. It's not the building that's worth five times more money; it's the land.

The main reason why land is worth more is that it is subject to more intense economic activity and because of the circular shape of hubs, the center area is subject to the most activity. So, land prices go up in the middle.

Now, because the center of a circle will never grow, the land here is very scarce. Think of a slice of pizza. If you make the pizza larger, by only a centimeter, there is lots of pizza added on the crust, but the point of the pizza slice does not change in size. The same is true when cities grow. The outside ring of land has way more area, than the center. So, land on the outside ring is more affordable.

Since land in the city becomes more expensive, the lots are used more intensively, with little green space left, and buildings are built as tall as necessary and feasible.

This is why you see office towers, and apartment buildings, rental units, or condominium units, built in the city.

Is it really worth spending millions on a small plot of downtown land, when there is so much available land in the countryside?

If you can fit more people in a building, then yes, it is.

Let's put some numbers into an example to make sense of this.

Let's use two same-size lots, one located in a central location, and another in a suburban one. In each location, the lodgings will be of the same value per household, which means the same quality of materials and amenities. In this case we are talking about a lodging unit with a modern kitchen, 2 bathrooms, and 2 bedrooms.

TABLE 1
Suburbs vs Cities

Location	Suburb	City
Size of lot	50x100 = 5,000 sq ft.	50x100 = 5,000 sq ft.
Price	$50,000	$1,000,000
Price per sq ft	$10	$200
Value of lodging per unit	$300,000	$300,000
Number of units	1 house	20 apartments
Value of the real estate	$350,000	20 X $350,000 = $7,000,000
Commute distance	30 km	1 km
Commute time	1 hour transit	12-minute walk

In this example, a household can choose between equivalent investments in terms of real estate. The arbitrage is between living space and proximity to the city. The urban setting imposes a less intimate lifestyle with less space, which is countered by a walkable commute to work and city activities such as theatres and restaurants. The suburban setting offers a more intimate lifestyle with more personal space, including a home office, several parking spots and a yard. This is countered by a longer transit commute.

Now, this example is static; it does not predict changes in land values over time. To explain that, we must use some basic economics: supply and demand.

Supply and Demand for Land

I know, you don't buy land, you need a house to live in. But we have to start with land values.

First, the suburban option.

Because of the concentric form of cities, there is always more land away from the city, than in the center. Think of a pizza slice. The larger the slice, the more crust.

But the point of the slice always remains the same size. This means that the supply of land in suburban areas is relatively elastic. Most cities are surrounded by farmland or neighboring villages that can easily accommodate an expansion of population.

In this case, an increase in demand for commuter neighborhoods, as the city economy grows and attracts workers, would not generate a large increase in the value of homes in the outer rings of suburbia. This said, the increase in demand would generate an increase in both the quantity supplied of land, and of housing units. There would not be a shortage of housing. And this housing would probably be affordable, notwithstanding the long commute to work.

FIGURE 1
Supply and Demand of Land in Suburban Settings

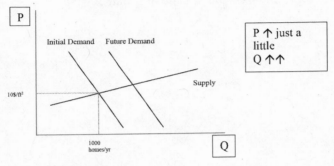

P - Price; Q - Quantity

Second, the urban option.

Because of the concentric form of cities, there is always less land in the center, than away. This means that the supply of land in urban areas is rare, or scarce, or both (they mean the same thing). Therefore, supply of land is inelastic.

Once land is built up in the city, it is off the market for resale, unless its owner wishes to relocate, which may not be the case at any given time. For producers, the advantages of central land are many: lower transportation costs by locating close to suppliers, available labour pool and distribution networks. Other advantages include lower tacit information costs (easier to network at the local pub), knowledge spillovers and proximity to specialized services.

Since the land is rare, any increase in demand will "ride up" the steeper supply curve, and result in higher prices.

FIGURE 2
Supply and Demand of Land in Urban Setting

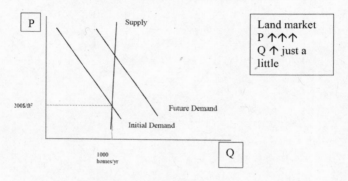

Now, this explains land prices, but does not answer the question of the quantity of lodging units.

Supply and Demand for Housing

There are basically two options for urban land use (I am trying to keep things simple here).

The first option is for the ultra-rich to build single-family homes around the urban core. Every city has a neighbourhood of mansions.[1] Since the ultra-rich are the only ones to be able to afford high land prices, they could still be able to build a mansion in the city.

In this case, the higher prices would take in all of the increase in demand, and there would not be an increase in the quantity of housing units built. The houses are huge, but they still only house one household, or family, or whatever you want to call it. The only option for lower income households would be to live in the suburbs.

FIGURE 3
Supply and Demand of Single-Unit-Housing in Urban Setting

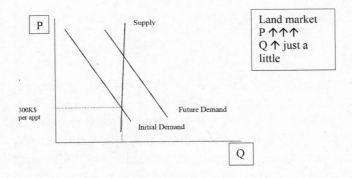

The second option is to build taller multi-family apartment buildings. In this case, the higher land prices are divided by the multiple tenants, or condominium owners, into affordable amounts. The higher land prices will, in this case, substantially increase the number of housing units.

So, should you buy a house in the city, a condo in the city, or a house in the suburbs? It's not for me to say, since these choices involve many other factors such as where you work, who you live with, and your lifestyle. If you would rather drive to the mall to buy some milk, maybe city life is not for you. If you

FIGURE 4

Supply and Demand of Multiple-Unit-Housing Units in Urban Setting

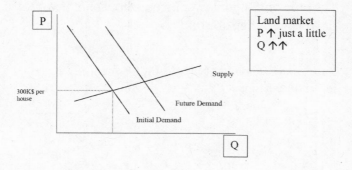

This being said, it is worth comparing the urban condo with the suburban home, since most of us can't afford the big house in the city. The following table compares the lifestyle impact on one's budget. The figures are simply indicative and may not reflect actual costs. Most of the condo-life savings are from foregoing the automobile.

As you can see, city life can have its advantages. Which one is a better investment? It really depends on the evolution of the city, and the neighbourhood, but keep in mind that in both these cases, the elasticity of land supply is flat. Which means it's pretty easy to build more homes in the suburbs. And it's just as easy to build taller condo towers in the city.

Generally speaking, the most lucrative investments are made in assets where supply is inelastic.

TABLE 2
Suburbs vs Condo, Costs

Costs per month	Suburban Home	Urban Condo
Mortgage and Taxes	$2,400	$2,400
Insurance	$100	$60
Hydro	$200	$80
Maintenance	$ 200	$200 (condo fees)
Commute	$100 (transit pass)	$0
Car, gas and insurance	$800	$260 (weekend rentals)
Total	$3,800	$3,000

SECTION 2

Jacobs' Urban Economics

In this section, we will discuss the economic principles that Jane Jacobs brings to the discussion. If you haven't noticed already, I am a big fan of Jacobs. If you don't know her, look her up! She's just really interesting.

I wouldn't say she's right about everything she ever wrote. But don't ask me to tell you what she's wrong about. I just love her work. I fell in love with her theory when I was in university, and my economics professors didn't really understand why at the time. They've mostly come around. She wasn't an academic, so many serious researchers kind of scoff at her writing. But really, I think she deserves a Nobel prize and mandatory reading status in the second or third year of any undergraduate degree in social science.

Jane Jacobs is mostly known for her contribution to urban planning. Her first book was a true *pavé dans la mare*, as we say in French. She had a fight to pick with the urban planners who designed the housing "projects" in New York City, and elsewhere, most of which became slums and miserable neighborhoods. People who think that the Bronx, and Brooklyn are cool today owe a lot to Jacobs. She forced policymakers to rethink planning with mixed-use and human-design principles. She won the urban planning fight with her landmark 1959 book *The Death and Life of Great American Cities*.

She does not get so much credit for her economics work, even though she thought that it was her most important contribution to public debate. Of course, there are now many economists who have come on board. The most important one was Robert Lucas, in the late 1980s, who was inspired by Jacobs to integrate human capital assumptions into a macro-economic growth model. Lucas was impressed with Jacobs but found it difficult to actually model her theories in the language of deductive mathematics. Other aspects of Jacobs' theories were discussed by important economists such as Edward Glaeser, Paul Romer, and Michael Porter. Her theories have also been adopted in the sub-field of Urban Economics as of the late 1990s.[1]

Still many economists have never heard of her. I believe that one reason for this is that most economists act as experts on policy for governments. And most governments don't follow the territory of a city-state, they mostly operate on the logic of nation-states, including both cities and rural areas.

Another reason is that most economists prefer to model the economy using lots of data, deductive logic, and mathematical techniques. Jacobs' work does not fit this methodology, since it is based on field observations and inductive logic. Jacobs' work is better appreciated if you consider that traditional techniques from the subfield of political economy are credible ways of understanding the economy.

CHAPTER 4

Jacobs' Theory of Import Replacement

Jane Jacobs' most important economic concept is, in my view, the idea of import replacement. This idea is at the core of what she describes as growing, innovative cities. This dynamic aspect of the economy is the heart and lungs of the economic system. Welcome to the land of Jacobs.

However, this concept is hard to model, hard to predict, and hard to nurture. It is hard to understand because we don't always have the specific data to analyse this core economic function. This is a radical theory which does help to understand cities, innovation, and prosperity. The theory was developed in Jacobs' second book, *The Economy of Cities*, published in 1969.

The theory holds on one key concept: a self-reinforcing feedback she called the "import-replacement cycle," which she documents as best one can, when no one else is measuring this phenomenon. This concept is the key to economic development, and so it is the foundation for other concepts that we will get to later.

Jacobs insists on referring to trade (exports and imports) between cities, as opposed to classical economists who refer to trade between nations, a habit that goes all the way back to Adam Smith.

In a nutshell, the idea of import-replacement is quite simple. You have an economy with a number of imported goods. Consumers are used to this, but somehow, an entrepreneur decides to locally-produce, to copy, an import. All of a sudden, and usually at a small-scale, citizens start consuming locally produced goods, instead of the imports. What was once imported from another city or region is now produced locally.[1]

Why do this?

Import replacements are usually better suited to the local market, provide appreciated variety to consumers, reduce transport costs, and are not subject to tariffs.

First, some imports may not be well suited to the local market. For example, American magazines are less appealing to Québécois readers for linguistic and cultural reasons. It is reasonable to see an opportunity for a local magazine market in Quebec, where most people speak French. Languages and cultural preferences are an important factor in import-replacement.

Second, consumers prefer variety in consumption.[2] Imports generally contribute to diversifying their basket of goods. The point of purchasing an item that needs extensive shipping is often to have access to a good which is substantially different than what is produced locally. Better yet, a replaced import is often modified to better suit local preferences. Consumers now have more choices because import replacement usually is done gradually. The new locally-produced goods do not replace all of the quantities of imported goods.

Third, imports may be overly expensive due to transport costs. For example, Asian-built cars are more expensive in Canada than cars built in Detroit, USA, or Oshawa, Ontario, because they need to be shipped halfway around the world. Shipping costs, when high, encourage import-replacement.

Finally, import tariffs increase the price of foreign products. For example, Canada imposes a set of tariffs on Chinese products. If the tariffs are high enough, the price differential makes it interesting for locals to purchase locally-produced substitutes.

How does this process actually work?

Before the import-replacement process begins, an economy must be able to afford the imports in the first place. Jacobs argues that most dynamic, and forward, cities start as successful regions due to the export of a specific manufactured good, or natural resource. The export revenue generates the capital needed to import consumption goods.

Let's run through a hypothetical example from a fictitious cattle supply region we will call Cattaliana.

Phase 1 – Successful export affords import
• Cattle exports generate foreign currency in the Cattaliana economy

- Wine imports are ordered and sent to Cattaliana
- Foreign currency is used to purchase the wine, from foreign sources
- Cattaliana households drink wine (maybe for the first time), and they seem to like it.

Phase 2 – Breakaway entrepreneur
- Local cowboy becomes a wine aficionado
- Local cowboy becomes frustrated in his career, and lack of advancement
- Local cowboy starts a side-hustle business, in winery
- Side hustle becomes full-time job. Cowboy quits his job, and breaks away from cattle ranch to launch a full-scale winery
- 5 percent of the wine imports are now replaced by local wine.

Phase 3 – Employment and Capital Multiplier
- Wine production is "new work," and creates local jobs
- Wine is sold mostly locally at first.
- Cattaliana starts to export wine to neighboring towns and cities, not abroad
- Wine industry employment grows, labour market income grows, aggregate demand for goods and services grows in general
- Wine exports (to neighboring towns) generate capital for Cattaliana economy.

Phase 4 – Cycle starts again, times three

- Successful wine sales create discretionary funds for the purchase of new types of imports
- Cattaliana households now import shoes, umbrellas, and books from foreign countries
- Breakaway entrepreneurs, encouraged by the bankers and the business community, substitute a share of the imports of shoes, umbrellas, and books, by local production
- Employment and capital grow as Cattaliana' s economy diversifies and expands.

We see the cycle has the potential to be self-reinforcing. Local entrepreneurs will probably be inspired by the first "breakaway entrepreneur" in their community and start to replace other imports with local production.

Of course, if local economic agents are content with their supply region status, they won't necessarily engage in import-replacement.

Diversity Feedback

It is important to note that import-replacement automatically increases the industrial diversity of the city. This has five positive effects on the economy.

First, diversity of local production reduces costs for most producers of old work. The city economy grows in scale, and scope. This means there are more inputs available locally, more specialized tools, machines, materials, knowledge, etc., which benefit producers in general.

Second, workers are not the same. Each worker has individual strengths, preferences, interests, and training. A greater diversity of local production therefore increases labour productivity by allowing a better allocation of labour according to individual strengths.

Third, diversity of local production also increases innovation opportunities, as different industries learn from each other. The transmission of knowledge is more important when different industries share the same banks, schools, and other specialized services.

Fourth, the export revenue generated by import-replacement brings a following of new and fresh imports. Remember that consumers prefer variety. When sailing in far-away places, shippers often pick up a wide range of foreign goods which may find a market back home.

Thus, the new import wave will bring a variety of novel wares. This means there can be a multiplier effect to import-replacement. As export revenue grows, so does the quantity and variety of imports. Hence, the opportunities to replace these imports multiply with each round of import-replacement.

Finally, industrial diversity reduces economic volatility. Industry cycles are smoothed over as their relative weight within the local system is reduced. A foreign demand shock for cattle in Cattaliana won't be as hard to take if the economy also produces wine and shoes.

Measurement

How can one observe the import-replacement phenomenon?

It is difficult to operationalize this type of variable. This is scientific jargon which means that it's hard to measure. Ready-made available data for city economies is not the first priority of government statistical agencies, although there has been incredible progress made in this field in the past 20 years.[3]

This being said, there are a few ways of doing it.

First, an anthropological-type study using fieldwork can be useful. By travelling in the city, interviewing entrepreneurs and bankers, one will be able to identify new work activities, and try to link them to previous imports. This is the kind of work that business journalists can also help with.

The researcher will look for activity in the core, but also to see if any workshops, or factories, have migrated to the city region, which includes suburban residential areas, and the immediate hinterland of the city. This is precisely the type of work Jacobs did in her books. She offers many examples of import-replacement. Unfortunately, the problem with this approach is that it is anecdotal and will be hard to associate directly with quantitative measurements, such as the balance of payments, GDP, patent activity, or industrial investment.

Second, one may have access to Export-Import data from a statistical agency that represents a metropolitan area. This is not possible in countries where the metropolitan area is engulfed within a much larger territory, such as the USA, France, Canada, China, etc. However, it is possible with data from city-states, such as Singapore. According to Jacobs' theory, bursts in exports would precede increases in imports. Imports would grow in both quantity and variety. These bursts in imports would then be followed by bursts of new-work exports. Studies on city-states can be useful to verify this hypothesis.

Exports and imports would be constantly catching up, and passing, each other, as both grow continuously. A trade deficit (X<M) would be associated with slow growth overall. But this is not a bad thing as the city recharges its batteries with fresh ideas from new imports.

A trade surplus (X>M) would be associated with a growth spurt, fuelled by new work as old imports are replaced.

A third measurement of this phenomenon would be to break down GDP figures by industry to try to see the apparition of new work in the data. This is difficult since "new work," which is truly innovative, is often poorly categorised by statisticians, and lumped into "other" categories. Another difficulty is the absence of detailed industry breakdowns for scarce "metropolitan" GDP data.

Making it Visual

Let's try to visualize the evolution of a growing city. We will start with the basic classical explanations and then add some of Jacobs' theory.

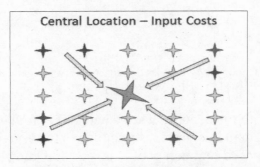

Central Location — Input Costs

A central location is chosen for regional production. It becomes a purchaser for small outlying suppliers.

On an equal footing, each village started out the same size. The one in the middle, however, started growing because of its ability to guarantee the lowest cost of production, due to its central location. Outer villages export their specialties to the center, who transforms each input into manufactured outputs. To be fair to all the villages, the government also built public services in the middle location.

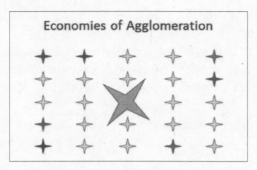

As the city grows, it generates economies of agglomeration,
attracting more producers.

With the benefits of scale which they find in the
city, small businesses thrive thanks to specialized
services, a common pool of labour and knowledge
spillovers.

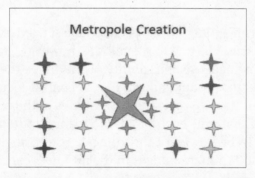

As the city grows, it expands into the neighboring villages.

The multiplier effect works its magic and as the
city grows, exporting to far-away foreign markets,
its local production increases, creating an outer-ring
of manufacturing and housing quarters.

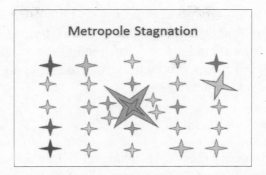

City-work leaves and is transplanted to low-cost production zones.

Due to lack of constant innovation and import-replacement, the city has not continued to re-invent itself. It loses legacy manufacturing to low-cost competitors overseas. Some products go out of production because they are obsolete. Business elites argue for lower wages to help compete, but the solution is elsewhere.

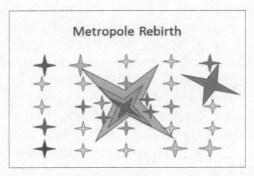

Cheap rent in the city attracts young entrepreneurs.

A new generation of young entrepreneurs take on the abandoned factories and warehouses and transform them into cool, hip, techno shops, developing the future production lines the city needs to re-invent itself and keep afloat.

Jacobs and Classical Economists

What would a classical economist like David Ricardo say about this theory? Ricardo is famous for arguing in favour of trade between countries, even if one country was more productive in all of the tradeable goods, than the other. Ricardo's argument is that the productive country was probably better at some of its productions. So, if you specialize trade, you minimize the opportunity cost of producing what you are not really good at making.

The problem is that these guys, including Adam Smith, probably held visceral views about the 'urban' factor. They probably took for granted that the economy was urban, because the countryside was so obviously less developed. However, both Smith and Ricardo wrote their theories of trade as being conducted by kingdoms, or states, or nations. They didn't factor in the city being the main importer or exporter of trade goods. This oversight has incredibly important consequences.

Jacobs (1985) of course criticizes both Smith and Ricardo for setting the philosophical foundations of economic theory purporting that economies should specialize and then trade. Jacobs does not propose to limit trade, quite the contrary. She saw a third way in this problem. Trade brings diversity and change to both countries' economies. She saw that cities are creating diversity, and she saw good in that.

Ask the Irish if specializing in potato production was smart. It was not smart. And it was not their idea, by the way.

Well, no one saw the potato failure coming, you might retort. It was smart while it lasted, you might say.

Well, maybe, but no. You should always diversify to protect your assets.

CHAPTER 5

City Instabilities

Cities are the heart and lungs of the economic system, but they have their weaknesses. Inherent built-in instabilities will eventually bring down even the world's most powerful cities. The worst part of this is that cities tend to create the problems that can bring them down.

Instability is a built-in mechanism that will cause disruptions in a system's path. For Jacobs, instabilities are built-in forces that will hurt an economy's capacity to innovate and grow.

Congestion, Pollution, and Crime

Cities that grow automatically generate congestion, pollution, and crime. These instabilities are the easiest to understand. As cities grow, they become congested, which increases transportation costs. The congestion can also lead to pollution, which also comes from the increased intensity of production on the land.

In older cities, overcrowding led to water pollution and poor sanitation. Nowadays, brine water (this is what you flush from your toilet) is treated, but congested roads still lead to air pollution today.

Economic agglomeration and population overcrowding can lead to increased crime levels. This is an important stress factor on cities, and may accelerate a decrease in economic activity into an irreversible decline. Of course, we have solutions to this, but if we had not, who would want to live in a city?

Labour Reducing Process Innovations

Being hotbeds of innovation, city economies not only invent new products, but also lead to improvements in production processes. Not only do cities invent new products, they also get old work done more efficiently. This is one of the negative aspects of Schumpeter's theory of "Creative Destruction."

Cities tend to invent machines, robots, automated technologies, electronics, etc., that reduce the number of workers needed. The unemployed were not incompetent, and their companies were not suffering from lack of sales. They were just made less attractive by new technology. Idle workers incur costs to the rest of society, such as retraining and income supplements. These resources could instead have been invested to improve the city.

Obsolescence

Another aspect of Creative Destruction is the generally inevitable obsolescence of what we produce. Goods are replaced on the market by a newer product. For example, the typewriter is no longer being produced as the new substitute of personal computers has made it obsolete.

Cities that produce soon-to-be-obsolete goods will feel the brunt of this drastic change in the economy.

Old-Work Transplants

When city work becomes mature, it tends to leave the city. By mature, we mean that new production usually goes through phases of innovation, where with time, the processes become defined and improved, and where the product itself has gone though sufficient iterations to have found its final shape, size, weight, and overall design. Inventing new products is easier to do in the city, where there are some available spaces in workshops, where you can find an ecosystem of bankers and other specialists to help finance and develop the product.

But once the product reaches a stage of maturity, the original producers are often faced with stiff competition and need to seek cost reductions so that they can stay in business. Leaving the city usually helps to do that. Outside the city, whether in a small town located not too far, or in a faraway country, companies seek lower land and labour costs.

The work is transplanted.

This is an important aspect of Jacobs' theory, because it underscores the importance of cities as inventors and developers of new goods and services. But this innovative capacity is also a cause for instability. When the new work becomes mature and leaves the city, workers are left without jobs, and real estate is left empty.

Of course, the towns that receive the transplanted work will feel immediate economic growth and benefit from new sources of income. Meanwhile, the city that invented this work has to reinvent itself. Jacobs argues that this process is truly universal and applies to all urbanized civilisations throughout history and across the planet. I think that any reader from anywhere in the world can think of places that fit this description.

CHAPTER 6

Cities and Nation-States

Cities don't just create their own problems. Sometimes their problems are created by the political and economic environment they have to deal with. Being part of larger political structures, either unitary nation-states, federations, or confederations, imposes constraints and skews feedback mechanisms that can actually deter city growth.

Unfortunately, the incentive structures in political institutions often act to counter the flow of productive investment which can help cities solve their issues and develop their economy. This can happen with non-productive capital outflows from cities, or with the skewed feedback imposed by larger monetary unions.

Non-productive Capital Outflows

City economies are not independent of social, political, and cultural phenomena. Jacobs argues that cities may be negatively affected by non-productive capital outflows if they are part of larger nation-state countries, or worse, federations and confederations.

The higher-order government, whether central, or federal, will impose taxes on streams of personal income, corporate earnings, and consumption expenditures, wherever it is located. The strong cities will end up paying most of the levies but may not be enjoying most of the related spending.

On top of that, governments are not always good at investing money productively. I personally believe that governments are capable of productive investment. The issue is whether or not that capability is executed properly. Many businesspeople will concur that bureaucracy is an ill that also affects private corporations and is not exclusive to the public sector.

To be clear, financially speaking, a productive investment is an expenditure that generates a higher return. Economically speaking, productive investments will generate more capacity to produce, whether it's through the purchase of physical capital (machines and robots), or the improvement of labour productivity (training and education).

Now we must note that most of the typical government work (Regalian functions), such as the justice system, including contract, real estate, and patent tribunals, are crucial to the existence of market economies. Jacobs argues that governments tend to prefer "largesse" expenditures, aimed at redistributing wealth across the land.[1] As much as these programmes are sound on a moral level, or a political level, they do tend to transfer funds from the city to benefit poorer, more backward regions. For example, when governments build roads in rural areas, they usually need to pool the money from the larger territory because that particular area may not have the capital to build the road otherwise. The same is true for any government services such as postal services, health care, education, transportation, justice, and policing.

This is obviously a controversial statement. Most people won't appreciate being told their economy is backward. But if your local economy is dependent on transfers from other regions, then guess what, it is not a 'forward' economy. Again, this issue affects most parts of the world, on all continents.

Government regulations of crucial "club good" industries can also be detrimental to larger cities. For example, price regulations impose "national" prices to letter postage services, airfare, train service, telephone companies, and television distribution companies. Jacobs uses an example from Canada: the federal government granted a monopoly to the Bell Telephone Co. at the turn of the 1900s. In exchange for this, Bell was expected to service all of Canada, including rural areas, at no extra charge to the consumer. Urban dwellers ended up paying higher prices on telephone services to subsidize rural Canadians.

Jacobs argues that lower prices in Montreal and Toronto would have left money in these cities, which—probably—could have found more productive uses. Of course, proponents of national unity will argue that this is a small price to pay to keep the country together. It is certainly an important issue in a huge country like Canada, as opposed to what that debate would look like in a city-state like Singapore.

National Currencies

When Jacobs realized the importance of city trade for the creation of new work, she then realized that a city currency can greatly enhance the trade feedback. A city currency will smooth over business cycles, especially if they are related to inter-city trade.

Again, this is the kind of radical thinking that some policymakers can't bear. I understand fully because large countries would much prefer to have a centralized currency, than to have exchange rates within the same country. For most people, money and country are almost synonyms. It's worth discussing the theory, though. If this is important for a healthy economy, then we should at least consider it.

When a city has a trade deficit (Exports < Imports), it could fall into a recession. However, a free-floating city currency would depreciate as demand for the local currency decreases relative to the demand for foreign currency. This depreciation usually happens before production levels are affected. This will bolster the foreign price of city export goods without affecting local prices and wages.

This is classic economics. But Jacobs is applying it to the city-level of political geography, not the state.

Foreign demand for the city currency would be perfectly aligned with that city's exports. In a stable-state model, economists are looking for an equilibrium that clears markets. But Jacobs goes a step further, and thinks of the system as a dynamic ecosystem, open to change. With trade comes import-replacement, and a new industrial structure.

She insists on the importance of exchange rates as a feedback mechanism. Feedback is information, she writes. It's really quite brilliant.

And it's not clear to me why macroeconomists don't see it so clearly. Their colleagues, microeconomists, constantly chant the advantages of prices as a 'signal' mechanism, another way of saying information feedback.

Economists do see exchange rates as a feedback, but mostly to balance international payments, so that the capital investment flows don't overpower the tradeable goods flows.

Jacobs argues that city exchange rates are useful because city entrepreneurs need that information to make decisions about production and trade. It's a price-signal about inter-city, and international markets. The more information they have access to, the better their decisions about future production, imports, and exports.

The feedback information of the exchange rate with other currencies is therefore perfectly useful information for the city economy.

Inversely, when a city has a trade surplus (Exports > Imports), it could go into overheating, which generates inflation. On strong foreign demand for city exports, the city currency will appreciate, making the exports even more expensive. This will have two effects.

First, exports sales will slow down, reducing inflationary pressures from shortages on factor markets, such as the job market, or the steel market.

Second, the city's purchasing power for imports will rise. This will fuel a new round of importing, which—hopefully—will in turn feed a new round of import replacements.

Some city-states still exist. And they are some of the fastest-growing economies in the world. Singapore is a fastest-growing city-state that has insisted on using a local city currency.

Few economies still use city currencies. Most states have "nationalized" currency printing under a central bank. According to Jacobs, this has concentrated the currency trade information feedback on the largest, incumbent cities, of their nation. Hence, many countries now have only one large dominant city (ex: Paris, France, London, UK, or Milan, Italy).

There are many reasons why countries end up with a dominant city, and most economists won't say it's because of the currency system.

Another problem with national currencies is that it may exacerbate the tensions between two regions of the country, whose economies are very different. For example, if you have an important natural resource supply region in one part of the country, and a diverse metropolis in another part of the country, the trade patterns of those economies may not be synchronized at all. In Canada, the CAD/USD exchange rate was very high for many years because of the strong demand for Alberta oil. The Canadian dollar is notorious for moving in direct correlation with the price of oil. Many people called it a petrodollar.

Jacobs argues that this is actually hurting the urban areas, whose economies are not based on natural resources, but on manufacturing and services.[2]

Until the past century however, Jacobs (1985) argues, most currencies in human history were city currencies. Imperial currencies have existed, but many empires tolerated and encouraged city currencies within their military realm.

The European Union did not follow Jacobs' advice when they created a continental currency in 2000. They eliminated their national currencies to merge them into the Euro. Advantages of a Currency Bloc include lower transaction costs across borders, elimination of exchange rate risk and increased political integration mitigating the future possibilities of war within Europe. This project was a long-time coming, being a dream of German and French leaders for centuries, such as Napoleon. Most economists now agree it was a mistake, and the regions who have fallen behind Germany, such as many areas of France, Spain, Portugal, Greece, and Italy are suffering from a stultified economic system.

This kind of economic discussion really leads to some discomfort for many people, who really love their country. They've been told that they live in a great country, and what can we respond to that?

But you have to admit that large countries like Canada, Brazil, USA, South Africa, Congo, Russia, China, or India, on its face, are a hard sell. When you think of their sheer size, of the Indigenous Peoples, the different ethnic, linguistic, and cultural groups, I don't think you could convince someone that a social project like this would be an easy proposition.

There are serious issues in these countries about who gets the resources, and how they are distributed across the population. Indigenous Peoples in particular would benefit from a better deal. They probably wouldn't disagree with the idea of having several currencies in the country, especially if it could help their economies, notably in isolated areas where prices for food and goods are incredibly high.

SECTION 3

Jacobs' Spectrum of Economic Regions

In this section, we will discuss Jacobs' categorizations of economic regions. This is really useful when you are trying to figure out if an economy has a bright future, or if it is vulnerable to challenges.

This is important information if you are planning on moving into a new town, or a city, and investing your time and energy into that economy's future.

Buying a house in Detroit in 1910 was a promising move, when the city was inventing the modern automobile. Buying a house in Detroit in 2010 was a bold move, when the city was suffering from its lack of diversification and shrinking auto sector. Crime was rampant and, in many neighborhoods, most homes were abandoned.

To compare Detroit yesterday with today, we are going to classify economies along a spectrum. A spectrum is an axis that follows one variable. It usually is a continuous axis, which starts at one extreme, and ends at another extreme. Sometimes, the axis has no boundaries, and runs to infinity.

In this case, we will compare cities on the axis of the dynamic nature of their economy. We will place them on the spectrum according to their capacity to be dynamic economies, capable of innovation and adaptation, or not

Jacobs' (1970, 1980, 1985) theory explains how city-economies adapt to each other, in relation to geography, trade, government, and business forces. She presents six types of economic regions. I am taking the liberty in this text to rename some of them for clarity. If you look for this classification in her books, you will probably do some jumping from one chapter to another. I've re-organized these concepts to make them easier to understand.

The six regions are: the Forward City, the City Region, the Entrepot City, the Supply Region, the Transplant Region, and the Backward City.

These categories are presented from one extreme to another, from the most dynamic (Forward City) to the least dynamic (Backward City).

Jacobs's categories of economies are constructed from her own theory of economic growth, which is grounded in her visits to cities across the globe, but also in her review of economic history, anthropology, and a critical evaluation of macroeconomics.

The six categories are differentiated according to variables such as density, industrial diversity, resource endowment, company size, the import-replacement function, product innovation, process innovation, employment, price levels, and immigration patterns.

CHAPTER 7

The Forward City

A "Jacobs Agglomeration" is a city which is diverse, growing, and inventive.[1] It is an inductive conclusion based on several criteria (rather than a deduction, based on assumptions). Such a city tends to create opportunity for migrants and youth, tends to invent new products and industries, and tends to be very open to trade and science.

We will call these economies "Forward Cities" for their unique capacity to constantly innovate, generate new products, and adapt smoothly to changing trade patterns. This quality is what makes Forward Cities the economic heart and lung of the rest of the system, and provides technology improvements, and prosperity to many other economies.

Economic literature now uses the term Jacobs' agglomeration, and the term "forward city" is original to this text. It serves to illustrate the economic development quality of these cities, and to differentiate them from "backward cities", since they are opposites on the Jacobs spectrum of economic regions.

Forward cities can be large or small. But they do grow rapidly at some point in time. Most of them are now quite large and are thus often dubbed as a "metropolis," or "economic capital."

Jacobs identifies Detroit, of 1910, as an example of a forward city. The density of Detroit at the time was relatively high, compared to smaller rural settlements of that period. The city was then bustling with hundreds of car design and manufacturing companies, a new industry that was in a phase of rapid development and expansion.

The industrial diversity of the city was growing at the time, as Detroit was replacing German automobile imports with local production.

As with most forward cities, the geographic location of Detroit did not confer any particular resource endowments such as minerals or oil. As the name of the city indicates, the city was a natural location for a maritime port although set well inside the North American continent, it has a natural link between Great Lakes waterways. The city was also at the hub of road transportation between the US Midwest and Southern Ontario.

In the 1800s, the city's economy grew. Jacobs mentions Detroit's role in the flour industry, which was rapidly industrializing as milling and food processing became mechanized. Detroit was exporting flour all around the Great Lakes, so it somehow added shipbuilding for the transportation of its flour and food products. Machinists from the flour mills probably added the new work of maritime engine-making, according to Jacobs.

Economic history literature indicates that by 1910 Detroit hosted a variety of small and medium sized automobile companies. It came to be known as "Motor City" for this reason. Of the 300 car-makers,[2] and thousands of parts companies, the industry eventually consolidated into three large multinationals (GM, Ford and Chrysler) whose headquarters are still in or around Detroit.

According to Jacobs, Detroit's growth is due to its "import-replacement." Detroit did not invent the automobile, which was a German invention. However, Detroit was the catalytical birthplace of this industry in North America, and greatly contributed to the refinement and improvement of both the product, and its production process.

This led to a strong demand for labour, and high employment in the city. This attracted people to the city, whose population grew.

The exports of cars enabled the city to import many higher-order goods, and the wider variety of local production helped keep overall prices low. The price of cars themselves was continuously decreasing, as the technology and processes improved, and as scale increased.

Instabilities associated with forward cities are:
- Unaddressed congestion, pollution, crime
- Eventual loss of work to lower-cost regions
- Obsolescence
- Capital withdrawals from nation-state policy
- National currency.

Risk factors associated with forward cities are:
- To gradually stop import-replacing
- To stop locally innovating.

What can governments do to help these economies?
- Provide positive feedback mechanisms such as city currency
- Avoid non-productive capital outflows by nation-state
- Invest in productive investments such as new products, and science
- Encourage Breakaway Entrepreneurship
- Address pressing problems of urban life. Solutions may become opportunities to invent new industries.

CHAPTER 8

The City Region

Growing cities have a direct impact on their surrounding areas, often rural at first and sparsely populated. Analysts now speak of the "Greater XYZ City Area," or of Metropolitan Areas, which include "Outer Suburban Rings."

Once the metropolis grows outside its initial borders, these areas become engaged in the intricate network of the city economy. Their production diversifies as old work is transplanted outside the now congested core city. City regions directly benefit from the inventiveness of the core city, without having to deal with the congestion and pollution.

The density increases but remains low. The industrial diversity can be very high, surprising to many. The structure of this economy remains diverse in production, scale, and scope. The area does not need any particular natural resource endowment, other than land to build factories, houses for workers and their families, and office space for specialty service industries.

The area is indirectly engaged in import-replace-ment, which is due to its integration with the city economy. City regions can be product innovators or not. This is because producers transplant production here to save on costs, not out of a creative need to constantly invent new products.

Thus, these producers are very much interested in cost-saving process innovations, especially labour-saving technology. The employers here use more machines, automation, and robots, which increase the capital-labour ratio.

Ironically, the level of employment can be high and growing, which attracts migration from other regions, further out from the city.

Price levels tend to be low, as cost-saving measures, and diversity of local production, are the norm.

Instabilities include:
- The eventual loss of work to lower-cost regions
- A reduction in arrival of new work from a decline of the city
- Obsolescence
- Capital withdrawals from nation-state policy
- National currency

Policy prescriptions:
- Agree to what is best for core city.
- Invest in cost-cutting process innovation.

CHAPTER 9

The Hub/Entrepot City

If you understand the central location model, you will understand this category, and most people understand cities this way. These are locations that concentrate activity, which allows the city to provide larger scales of production, lower prices, and a wider availability of product.

One example of this is warehousing and distribution services to a larger region. This function exists in all cities that attract customers from outside its direct hinterland. Another example is the provision of larger-scale public services such as college education, hospitalisation and advanced health care, and higher courts of justice.

For example, some people come to the central city to shop for niche items, such as luxuries, which may not be available in their own cities in the same variety, quality, and price. Another example is large furniture stores which can attract clientele from hundreds of miles away.

Also, these cities are able to develop smaller segments of a market and provide an environment where business owners can thrive on a specialty offering. This creates a positive feedback for the city as people from surrounding areas will travel to consume, rather than buy in their own villages and towns. While they are in the city, they will probably look around to see what else is available. As you can imagine, many of these shopping trips are planned in advance, especially for households travelling a long distance.

The city ends up with an important supply of retail and intermediate goods which are warehoused. The risk of holding stock is reduced because the city's market is actually larger than its local base of residents.

A commonly used term is Entrepot cities, which Jacobs refers to in her books. This term is used for cities whose role is to warehouse export product from a nearby supply region, as it is waiting to be transported to other markets. For example, in the colonial period of New France and British North America, Montreal was an Entrepot city in furs, which were collected from all over North America, and warehoused in Lachine over the winter and spring, and then shipped to Europe in the warm season. Another example is Hong Kong, and Singapore, which the British Empire used as warehouse locations for their trade activities in Asia. Most of the colonial trading posts worldwide function as Entrepot cities.

Entrepot cities differ from Hub cities because they are not necessarily centrally located inside the country. They are usually located at the junction of land and sea, or at least at the junction of two important modes of transportation. This location allows them to funnel production to their warehouses which are close to a port, and then become exports when ships sail in. The logic of minimizing transport costs still applies, but the geography is tweaked by the types of modes of transportation implicit in international trade.

Public services usually follow the logic of a central location within the territory, because the services, such as education, or health care, are not subject to trade.

To many, it makes sense to locate both the commercial hub and the public service hub in the same city, making the investments in roads and infrastructure worthwhile. The public and private sectors are also complementary to each other as businesspeople need public services such as the courts of law to settle litigation, and an educated and healthy labour force to help produce their goods and services.

Entrepot cities will show steadiness in macro variables and may not grow past the scope of their broad hinterland. They may engage in intense trading but will not necessarily become a place of large-scale manufacturing.

Instabilities include:
- Technical change in product delivery and source
- National currency
- Foreign demand variation of hinterland production.

Policy prescriptions:
- Encourage import-replacement, and manufacturing
- Invest in cost-cutting process innovation.

CHAPTER 10

The Supply Region

Many Supply Regions—also known as resource economies—are quite wealthy, as they are usually endowed with a highly demanded natural resource.

However, Jacobs argues they are inherently fragile, and lack a capacity to adapt to changes in trade patterns. She qualifies them as being "backward" economies, along with Transplant Regions and Backward Cities.

An example of a Supply Region near Detroit is the Ohio iron ore region, which saw the rise of the Cleveland Cliffs mining company. Naturally endowed with a key mineral for making steel, widely used in making automobiles, the rise of the Detroit economy created what Jacobs calls a solvent market for Ohio's iron ore, and steel foundered in Cleveland. The mining area of Cleveland Cliffs is not a densely populated area, and its economy is highly concentrated in iron ore mining. Without the iron ore, one can wonder how much economic activity would take place there.

The mining industry is typically consolidated, made up of a few large companies. They are content with supplying other regions and do not engage in import-replacement. Generally, they are not known for product innovation.

Supply regions are therefore focused on reducing production costs and improving processes. The job market can grow at first, but usually is very stable or declining as labour-reducing technology is introduced.

Prices can be high as most consumer goods need to be imported. However, in this case, Ohio mines are relatively close to important cities such as Detroit and Cleveland, so prices here would be relatively low.

Migrants would be attracted to the area when the mines are being constructed, but immigration would be halted after their normal operations level off.

Supply regions that are struggling often find a way to receive funds from wealthier supply regions, or from wealthier forward cities.[1] These capital injections may not be economically productive, as they can generate a disposition of dependence toward wealthy areas. Politically, the transfers may be argued to be moral, but many economists believe these transfers contribute to keep poor regions in poverty.

Another structural problem that supply regions may face is being part of a currency union with other supply regions specialized in different industries.[2] The exchange rate will follow the trends of the industries with the largest trade volume, and these patterns may not help the smaller supply regions.

Instabilities:
- Capital injections from nation-state policy
- National currency disconnect.

Risk factors are:
- Foreign demand shocks
- Foreign recession shock
- New competition from lower-cost region
- Foreign substitute good shock
- New production substitute that leads to population clearance.

Policy prescriptions:
- Diversify industrial base to reduce foreign demand risk
- Avoid monopsony power on local labour that discourages breakaway entrepreneurship
- Invest constantly in cost-cutting process innovations.

CHAPTER 11

The Transplant Region

This type of economic region is similar to the Supply Region in many ways. However, its inception and its geography occur differently.

The Transplant Region is brought to life by the transfer of work from a congested city to a lower-cost production area. Its role is to supply cities and other regions with a specialized product.

However, its economic raison d'être has nothing to do with natural resources. It can be anywhere on earth, as long as transport and labour costs are lower than in the city.

Under the umbrella of the Detroit automobile industry, a city such as Flint, Michigan, is a perfect example of a Transplant Region. This is also known as a "company town" when the main employer is large and overwhelming. This main employer holds monopsony power on the local labour market.

Flint is where General Motors (GM) was created in 1908, an automobile consolidator that swallowed Buick and Chevrolet, along with dozens of other

Detroit-based carmakers. GM had decided to set up in Flint to avoid the high costs of the then bustling Detroit. The city was less than two hours away, so GM could bring workers over to this specialized area and continue to benefit from knowledge spillovers from the Detroit economy.

As most Transplant Regions, the city never diversified out of car making. GM eventually built its headquarters in Detroit, but Flint remained a key manufacturing location for a long time. However, lower-cost locations appeared over the last century and eventually Flint lost one plant after the other. Finally, in 1999, GM decided to shut its last plant in Flint, which made large Buick sedans that had gone out of fashion with SUV-craving consumers.

The population density of Transplant Regions is usually low, on purpose, to reduce overall costs of living, wages, and transportation.

At first, the absence of industrial diversity is not a problem, as this large, single-company, transplant comes "out of nowhere." It is seen as a "godsend" by local townspeople of a previously poor region. However, over time, the region may lose this work as the factory is transplanted again, to an even lower cost region.

A Transplant Region usually does not engage in import-replacement because the local employer is alone, very large, and dominates the political and economic culture of the region. This kind of monopoly on the labour market is called a monopsony, and research indicates they tend to discourage breakaway entrepreneurship and any form of competition for local labour.

The factory's strategic management decisions are not made locally; they come from a headquarter located outside the region. In this case, GM's Flint plants would follow orders from Detroit. Local initiative is limited to process innovations, and product innovations are not expected. If foreign demand is strong, the transplant region will enjoy growing demand for labour, and worker migration toward the region.

Risk factors are the same as for supply regions.

CHAPTER 12

The Backward City

To be dubbed "backward" is insulting. Jacobs actually writes that most cities in the world, and throughout history, are a backward economy. The good news is that a Backward City can evolve into a more forward economy.

Most people would say a backward economy is in decline or is non-competitive. They may be shielded from other, more competitive economies, by subsidies, import tariffs, or other barriers to trade. They probably had a golden age when an important natural resource, or a manufacturing facility was in its prime. That time is gone and now these places usually need capital transfers from central political institutions to maintain services.

Modern-day Detroit has definitely gone through a backward economy phase. In the 2000s, its population was declining, neighborhoods were abandoned, and houses were boarded up. When poverty and crime become rampant it is difficult to live with, especially in high-density cities in decline.

The size of companies tends to vary within a backward economy. In the case of a declining city, many large companies have probably left, leaving a gaping hole in the fabric of the economy. In the case of stagnant small towns, companies are generally small and not growing.

This city is not import-replacing. It is not inventing new products. It probably is not very good at process innovations either. Because of all this, consumption goods need to be imported at a high price, and the non-competitive local producers' output is overly expensive.

A note: Jacobs insists that price levels must be considered as relative to local wages. A foreigner travelling to a stagnant city may find prices are lower than what he is accustomed to at home. But that does not mean the locals can afford these prices.

Jobs are scarce, and the population is declining. Survival depends more and more on the local stock of natural resources and less and less on trade and productive investment.

The risk for this type of regional economy is that things get worse before they get better. A population exodus can relieve the city of the strain of providing for everyone. Remittance from expatriated workers may become the only capital inflow to the city.

Jacobs recommends that these cities avoid direct competition with large dynamic economies. One strategy Jacobs proposes is to start to construct a local symbiotic network of workshops and small factories that replace low-technology imports. Think of local food products such as a craft brewery, locally made clothes, or a local bank promoting local gift certificates, which cannot be used outside the region. This new production usually can be sold to other, neighboring backward economies. Keep in mind that she wrote this in 1969. Given the advent of "globalization" which is a euphemism for giant leaps of transplanting work to Asia, South America and other low-cost regions, this strategy is simply not quite as feasible in the 2020s. However, repatriation of manufacturing is not impossible and should be considered.

Another strategy that Jacobs proposes is to invest massively in culture. Having a differentiated culture often allows a rationale for import-replacement. Investing in the arts, sports, music, and theatre may lead to economic avenues which would be difficult to foresee. The beautiful thing about culture is that it is unique and cannot be transplanted halfway around the globe because a capitalist found a lower-cost labour market.

A strategy that is quite common for these types of economies, and that Jacobs is critical of, is to over-invest in tourism, especially as a last-ditch effort to save a struggling economy. Jacobs believes that tourism is an export, although it is not reported as such in national accounts. Her view is important here because she is essentially focussing on currency flows in and out of a region. Tourism is very much like an export because it serves out-of-town clients, who purchase a service, rather than a good, with out-of-town currency. In terms of money flows, it is very much like an export. And like exports, either natural resources or manufactured goods, tourism is very much subject to wild variations in exterior demand. Maybe even more so than export goods. Tourism is a fickle business, with high expectations in terms of fixed capital expenditures. Hotels and infrastructure are expensive to build and depreciate rather quickly. Modern mass tourism avails customers with enormous amounts of information on new destinations. The industry is thus subject to trends and the allure of novelty. If your region is not already known for its touristic virtues, Jacobs argues that this is a tricky strategy to adopt.

SECTION 4

Cities as a Dynamic Economy

In this section, we will discuss in more detail how cities actually change our lives, change our economies, change how we work, and change the products that we consume. This change is the dynamic element that is often missing from standard economic theory.

CHAPTER 13

Innovation in Jacobs' Agglomerations

Jacobs' agglomerations don't just replace imports, they also nurture product and process innovations. This is the key to understanding the geography of Schumpeter's Creative Destruction. Innovation is mostly urban.

But how does innovation affect the economy?

Mostly through development of new work, and new products, argues Jacobs.

But isn't economic development the same as economic growth?

No.

Jacobs makes a clear distinction between development and expansion. When they occur, they both can be the reason for an increase in total output. When Gross Domestic Product (GDP) grows, it may be because of development and/or expansion.

Development, on one hand, is when a system becomes more complex, when it adds functions and capabilities, and produces a wider variety of objects and services. Expansion, on the other hand, is when a system increases its output, without complexifying or adding new work. Expansion is more of the same.

So why don't economists use these ideas? Why isn't innovation better understood in economics?

There might be a few reasons for this. First of all, it is very difficult to measure economic development as opposed to expansion. When you look at GDP figures, they won't be broken down into categories which can help us determine if the economy is developing, or expanding, or both. Second, there is much prosperity to be gained from expansion, which is a much more palatable concept. If the mine expands, the town will prosper. If the mill grows, so will the economy. What's good for GM, is good for America.

The distinction is still quite valuable because expansion has its limits. To keep growing, economies need to develop, and diversify their production. One way to develop is to replace imports. Another way is to invent new work.

Jacobs (1969) argues that cities are natural environments for economic change because imports come through cities. This is because cities are usually located around ports and other transport hubs. Cities can afford to import new and innovative goods from foreign economies with the money earned from their exports.

But who invents the new things in the first place?

Cities, answers Jacobs.

Jacobs theorizes that cities invented almost everything that came to a market. Even agriculture and farming technologies.

It's a bold statement.

But the idea has made its way into academic discussions. Until the 1970s, historians and anthropologists thought that ancient (and modern) cities weren't possible without an agrarian surplus. So, farming had to have been invented before cities.

But Jacobs thought about how cities invent and solve so many problems. She concluded that cities may have invented farming.

How? No one knows exactly, even today. The earliest cities like Jericho did not leave detailed accounts of how they were built. We can only try to analyze the archeology.

If cities invented farming, they probably invented most other solutions to human problems, Jacobs proposes. I won't share all of her arguments here. I invite you to read her books for yourself. But if cities are so inventive, then how do they do it?

Jacobs has lots to say about that.

First, cities are a place of opportunity. This is where all the elements of a project can be found and brought together, whether it's materials, ingredients, tools, capital, workspace, or labour. That gets the ball rolling in a way that a truly rural environment cannot.

Second, cities exchange goods, and by doing so, they exchange ideas. When a city imports a new good, it is able to touch and feel a product it has never seen before. This interaction brought about by trade is usually so unremarkable that most economists don't consider it to be an important phenomenon.[1]

Country A makes something at which they are good. Country B makes something at which they are good. Country A and B increase their production by specializing and trading with each other. Everybody's happy.

Sounds great, and I see the logic of course. This is the Ricardian view. It's based in a comparison of opportunity cost that makes perfect sense... if the world does not change, ever.

But the world changes constantly, and this kind of simple modelling of trade does not take into account the flow of information that comes with trade.

Consider the previous example of office chairs (Chapter 2: Hub Cities). A share of the production will eventually be exported from the city as foreigners become aware of the existence of the product. This export brings in extra money to the city, which can use it to import goods from abroad. Let's assume the city imports fancy dinner chairs from abroad.

Most economists would believe this trade is a good thing, and these economies should specialize in the fields where they hold a relative comparative advantage. This is the Ricardo view.

Jacobs argues that instead of arguing over how the world SHOULD work, we should first try to look at how the world DOES work. She argues that most cities don't behave like the models.

Jacobs rather prefers to root her theory in observation, as opposed to deductive logic. She observes that cities tend to copy each other, to everyone's benefit. The first city has got wood, leather, and plastics. It can use the technique of "reverse-engineering" to copy the imported good and produce it locally. The import becomes a knowledge spillover between economies.

Further, the added local production also increases money stocks in the city, which enable its citizens to import more fancy products. This is a positive feedback loop directly related to trade.

Trade brings in new ideas to cities that often copy the imported products and thus increase their local production levels. Furthermore, Jacobs argues that cities use imports as inspiration. Ideas that are imported through trade, are the fuel of innovation. Imports fuel innovation.

This was a radical proposition for me when I first read it. In classical economics, imports are seen as a negative. They are substituted for national output, in the classic Keynesian GDP formula. This is a very static analysis of the situation. Of course, you can't say that your country made televisions, if they were shipped from a foreign country. We agree on that. But for Jacobs, imports are more than objects. They are full of new ideas, of new solutions that we might not have thought of previously.

So, you might object that Jacobs' theory does not apply to many imports, such as shipping coffee to Canada, a cold country that cannot produce coffee beans. That's true, and the ideas element in the coffee trade are not really quite important. Some tradeable goods are not so rich in knowledge spillovers.

But most of the value in tradeable goods is in complex objects, engineered precisely, and chock-full of intellectual capital. A tool is worth more money than its weight in coffee beans. That's because its economic value is greater. The more we transform resources, the more added-value to the cost structure and the more potential for information.

Consider the imported dinner chair example. There might be an assembly technique, a fancy carving, or a style, that the local producers have never seen before. The city might start producing dinner chairs, but it might also be inclined to use its creativity to invent a whole new type of chair, inspired by the fabrics, the assembly techniques, and the overall design of the imported good.

As producers act on the profit incentive, and as consumers love new, different, and better products, market-oriented cities become the natural location for inventive companies. The trade cycle generates a second positive feedback loop of invention and innovation.

CHAPTER 14

Diversity Trumps Specialization

Most Jacobs' agglomerations are typically very diversified economies. Think of Tokyo, London, Singapore, Shanghai, New York, San Francisco, Mexico City, Rio de Janeiro, etc.

These kinds of cities are now considered to be the engines of economic growth by modern macroeconomists. But this observable fact flies in the face of orthodox economic theory which argues that Ricardian comparative advantage should lead to economic specialization and increased production.

What does diversity mean?

Industrial diversity refers to the variety of goods and services which are produced in a city, a region, or a metropolitan area. It's not about diverse cultures, but diverse industries.

Some cities are very diverse. In the same city, you might find producers of food, chemicals, airplanes, pharmaceuticals, refined petroleum, cardboard, etc. You can also find local service providers such as TV, radio and print media, finance, insurance, law, accounting, health, and education.

Measuring concentration and diversity

You can measure economic diversity using a simple statistical technique. Economic geographers do this with the Location Quotient. Data for this has become more readily available in the past years. For example, the US Bureau of Economic Analysis provides data at the county, metropolitan and state levels, which makes it very easy to measure location quotients. The calculation is rather simple. You find the size of an industry in your area. You can use the number of jobs, or the total sales (GDP per industry). You divide by the total for the region. You do the same for that industry at the national level. Now you divide the regional share by the national share.

Location Quotient = Regional share of Industry X / National share of Industry X

The idea is to see if your region is over-represented, or more concentrated in a particular industry, than the country as a whole. If you live in a mining town, the mine will never be responsible for each job in the community. So, the location quotient will never be 100. But it does account for more jobs in your region, as a share of the regional total, than the weight that mining represents in the whole country. A location quotient above 2 is quite high. This means that your economy has at least twice the concentration in an industry, than the rest of the country.

This technique is useful for identifying highly specialized economic regions, such as mining areas, or economies that have developed a technical expertise, such as an aerospace cluster.[1]

As a rule of thumb, really diverse economies would have location quotients close to 1, for each sector of the economy, or at least a large number of these sectors. They would not have any location quotients above 1.2.

Advantages to diversity

Diversity has two main advantages, according to Jacobs (1970). First, it reduces vulnerabilities to foreign trends. Second, and more importantly, diversity increases innovation because science and technology spill over to different industries with greater ease when these industries share the same city.[2]

Solutions to technical problems can be useful in very different industries. For example, the clothing industry has come up with Velcro technology used in shoes and other garments. This technology has proven to be very useful in a wide array of industries, such as aerospace. Surprisingly, wings are attached to the fuselage of some planes with hard-pressed Velcro-type technology.

Jacobs' point is that in a diverse city, very different industries can learn from each other. In diverse cities, technology and knowledge will spill over more quickly from one industry to another. Innovation economists have dubbed this phenomenon cross-industry knowledge spillovers. Even though it is a difficult phenomenon to study empirically, it is generally accepted to be a factor. Even Alfred Marshall wrote about the magic in the air in an innovative city, where people learn from each other.

In the end, you can also ask yourself if diverse cities are wealthier than specialized regions. Sometimes they are. Sometimes they are not. Studies show that a Jacobs agglomeration typically grows at a steadier and more constant pace, which over time trumps the typically rocky path of high-flying resource economies. Manufacturing regions can be very prosperous, and are not as volatile as mining towns, but when they overspecialize, they inevitably collapse, and then they suffer tremendously.

Jacobs' agglomerations are more dynamic economies in the sense that they are more diverse and innovative than others.

Jacobs argues that trade will increase the strength of the hub city, as imports offer opportunity for new ideas. Cities often copy imports and produce them locally, adding to the local production level.

Jacobs' agglomerations tend to be more diverse because they invent new industries that add to previous activities. Jacobs argues this diversity is enviable because a) it protects the economy from violent foreign demand cycles, and b) it leads to cross-industry knowledge spillovers which generate more innovation and economic development.

Does this theory, which was developed in the 1960s, still apply today, in the 21st century? When

Jacobs wrote her books, New York City was still manufacturing clothes, machines, and furniture. Montreal used to produce toys, paint, and hardware for your kitchen.

What does New York City produce today? Well, a lot more media, like tv stations, but also video games. The manufacturing has been transplanted to many parts of the country and the world. So can this theory be useful? I answer that yes, I think it's still very useful. We still have to be creative, and invent new products, because if we don't, today's jobs will eventually be transplanted, and the economy will suffer.

And guess what, the creative jobs are in the cities. So, whether you are working on a new app, or an artificial intelligence software, you still need the feedback from your competition, you still need the tug-of-war of international trade. The city is still the place where you have most of that action.

I would add another point. A simple economic model proposed by the Austrian school of thought is of great use to illustrate the labour productivity gains to diversity in production. Jacobs argues that people are different, and that their talents can go idle if people are obligated to work in mono-industrial settings. This is especially true for couples who move to a new location, following one of the spouses' career opportunities. If you move to a coal town, and had training and a career as a film-maker, your only opportunities in this new town, where you probably don't have any personal contacts, might be to wait tables at a restaurant, or work the cash at the grocery store. If you had moved to a more diverse location, you would have better odds of finding work that suit your capabilities. This is also true for people who grow up in a mono-industrial town. A young person might have the talent to be a great chef, but if they don't want to sever personal ties with family and friends, they might take a job in the coal mine to support their family. That potential is going to waste.

In terms of the much-taught PPC model (Production Possibilities Curve), idle resources are not good for the economy, especially if the resource is labour. However, having a job does not mean your talents are used at their full potential. Jacobs' theory of diversity echoes the basic assumption of the PPC model that people are different, have different talents, and only when the economy produces at the most diverse possible combination of production, does the ultimate level of productivity become possible. The PPC model is taught in every first-term economics class, and never (to my knowledge) do these textbooks discuss the importance of diversity in local production to attain maximum output.

The economics of diversity are also embedded in classical microeconomics. If you consider "indifference curves" in consumer theory, which is a foundation of orthodox microeconomics, the model implicitly assumes that people prefer a variety of goods over a specialized basket of goods, even if the varied basket holds fewer items. This basic assumption is the foundation of microeconomics. And where do you find diversity of consumer goods? In cities.

Whether the academic field of standard economic thought wishes to acknowledge this or not, diversity matters, which is why cities matter.

CHAPTER 15

The Future of Montreal and 2nd-rank Cities

Montreal has a fascinating history. It was a major hub for Indigenous Peoples, known as Tiohtià:ke by the Iroquois (Haudenosaunee), and as Moonyang by the Algonquins (Anishinaabe). Montreal was one of the first industrialized cities of North America, the most critical settlement of New France, and the capital of British North America, which became the country of Canada. Over time, the city lost its first rank position to other cities, such as New York City and Toronto. However, given the cultural makeup of the city, its European flavour in North America, it will be a fascinating city to follow in the future. The city is well known for its nightlife, its festivals, and the French-Canadian joie de vivre.

Although she lived in Toronto, Jane Jacobs had many positive comments to make about Montreal. She liked that much of the city was built prior to the auto boom age, which meant that its density was higher than that of younger cities like Toronto. She also appreciated that expressways had been built up to, but not into the downtown core. In its later growth phase, Montreal avoided massive slum-clearance (to a degree) and preferred to rehabilitate poorer neighborhoods rather than raze them to the ground and rebuild high-end housing.

I would love to ask Jane Jacobs today what she thinks about all sorts of things. Of course, she passed away in 2006. I can only make educated guesses about how she would analyze our present-day economy. I have a hypothesis I would love to present to her. It is about these regional capitals, like Montreal, that are not the leading cities of their country. She was very explicit about Montreal in particular because she wrote a book in 1980, where she analyzed the economic position of the city in Canada, relative to the proposed independence movement in Quebec. She essentially wrote that if Quebec were to separate from Canada, it might happen that Montreal would find the social energy to develop itself as a truly dynamic city. If Quebec chose to stay in Canada, Montreal would suffer from watching, from the other end of highway 401, the growth of Toronto as the lead economic driver in the country. She also warned Quebecers about keeping the Canadian dollar, an issue I will discuss later in this chapter.

Of course, Quebec is still part of Canada, and Montreal has managed to grow at a reasonably healthy pace. No one would say that Montreal is booming, or the city of the future, or that its technological dynamism is astounding, but Montreal and Quebec have turned out to be the most reliable and economically sound parts of Canada in the last years. Montreal's unemployment rate is historically low, and its industrial base is enviably diverse and forward looking. Thanks to Montreal, the province of Quebec produces video games, pharmaceuticals, electric trucks, and private jets, and banks on high quality universities and healthy local financial institutions. Quebec also benefits from low-cost, green hydroelectricity it can sell to neighboring US states for a handsome profit.

While I agree with Jacobs that staying in Canada has stunted Montreal's development to a certain degree, and especially throughout the 1980s and 1990s, my analysis is that Montreal has more recently found a way to grow, *malgré tout,* in spite of important challenges such as not having a city-currency. This is also the case for many cities in the same situation, such as Birmingham, UK; Saint-Petersburg, Russia; and Cape Town, South Africa.[1] An example which is closer to me is that of a city that Montrealers love to hate: Boston, Massachusetts.

Being like Boston

We love to hate Boston, mostly because of the long-time rivalry between the cities. History books are littered with stories of the Boston Fenians who terrorized British loyalists, or of French-Canadian Coureurs de bois who hiked the Adirondack Mountains to

settle a score over a fur trade, or a woman. Those
relations prompted New Englanders to call the Seven
Years' War, the French and Indian War. When the
French-Canadian exodus of 1870-1890 was at its
peak, textile mills around Boston hired thousands of
our grandparents. The most famous Quebec strong-
man, in history, Louis Cyr, was born in Lowell,
Massachusetts.

Nowadays, the rivalry lives out mostly on hockey
rinks. It hurts me to think that Brad Marchand, a
fiery and gifted player, could have been French-
Canadian if his ancestors hadn't moved to the United
States. He could have worn the *Sainte-flanelle*, the
bleu-blanc-rouge, of the Montreal Canadiens hockey
club. I kid my students by daring them to wear a
Bruins jersey on the day of a test. Surely the Dean
will understand my position when the student com-
plains about failing the class.

Jokes aside, Montreal and Boston have a lot in
common. They are both majority Catholic settlements, with strong Irish, Italian and French com-
munities. They were both run by protestants for
a long time. But mostly, they have eerily similar
industrial structures. Boston and Montreal are hubs
of aerospace and military innovation industry. They
both are leaders in pharmaceuticals and medical
research.

They both have invested tremendously in their
university character. If young New Yorkers hold
Boston in high regard for Harvard, Yale, and MIT
universities, so do young Torontonians for McGill.

Of course, I don't wish to compare McGill University, whose funding is mostly public, to Harvard University, whose funding is private and seems to have no limits in its ability to charge for tuition. My point is that the second-city schools are a draw for the big-city students.

Another point in common is the fact that both cities have developed a strong financial district while it is obvious that the main financial activities of the country will lie elsewhere. In Boston, the financial industry was developed on the foundations of novel ideas such as mutual funds, and the insurance products of the Knights of Columbus social clubs. In Montreal, the financial industry was developed on the foundations of Quebec's linguistic difference. Discrimination towards francophone businesspeople led them to create French banks, which merged into the Banque Nationale, and the Mouvement Desjardins, a non-profit federation of locally-owned credit unions. Both of these financial institutions have grown tremendously in Montreal over the past century. Today, the Toronto banks hold less than 15 percent of the banking industry in Quebec.

My question for Jane Jacobs is this: if you are doomed by economic geography to be a second-tier city in your country, can you still be growing and developing?

I agree with Jacobs that it is always going to be harder for the second-tier cities of any country to harness the social energy needed to grow a "Jacobs Agglomeration." Analysts will argue that both cities (Boston and Montreal) have pursued a policy of encouraging high-technology clusters in targeted industries, which rely on strong university research, local venture-capital markets, and public support. Clusters contribute to agglomeration de facto. Fortunately, the cities have not slipped into long-term stultification, or become backward, in the face of the naturally stronger growth of their national counterpart, i.e., New York City and Toronto.

Harder, does not mean impossible. And having to struggle sometimes can be a boon.

Jacobs argued that the muddled economy of Birmingham, in the UK, far outgrew the much more impressive, and efficient, economy of Manchester over the 20th century. She attributed this to diversity of industry, and the smaller scale of workshops relative to the large plants in Manchester. Birmingham just had to keep muddling along, or else it lost ground. Manchester thought it was superior and neglected to nurture new sprouts of economic activity. Birmingham won.

The relationship between Montreal and Toronto, or Boston and New York City, are not quite the same as Birmingham and Manchester, since the main economic engine in the UK is obviously London. However, I posit that this idea of a local culture of constant project-building is quite important for any city, but especially for cities like Montreal and Boston. If the natural forces of the country's financial energies are concentrated elsewhere, you have to find another way.

One very Jacobsian phenomenon that has allowed Montreal to grow is the constant loss of work, due to transplants and obsolescence, over the past few decades. The city has lost all sorts of key industry, such as petroleum refining, paper production, pharmaceutical research, automobile construction, airplane building, and newspaper and magazine media outlets. In most parts of Quebec, these losses would have translated into massive unemployment. In Montreal, they've been absorbed almost seamlessly by new work in video games, social media applications, internet companies, electric vehicle production, and even artificial intelligence research companies.

If all this work had not gone, we probably would not have shifted our economy towards these forward-looking sectors. In Toronto, the shift is happening now, later in its history, because there previously wasn't a need to diversify the economy, especially out of the automobile industry, because it was so prosperous, for so long. Many people forget that southern Ontario was, and still is, a massive transplant economy in the auto-building sector. Since all of the companies are foreign (US, Japanese or Korean), few incentives exist to re-invest capital into the diversification of the greater Toronto area.

Future of second-rank cities

There are a few things that second-rank cities in any country can do to ensure their economic growth goes forward. Like every city, it should solve its problems. But second-rank cities have their own specific challenges. The first is to solidify the urban industries that are not so easy to transplant. Second, invest massively in transportation technologies. Third, invest in education and scientific research. Fourth, nurture the entrepreneurs and encourage breakaways. Fifth, look for transplants from the megapolises.

1. Urban industries

Some industries need to be urban. They don't necessarily need a large city, but they need all of the actors to be neighbors. They need the co-location of suppliers, customers, and competitors. Included here are haute-couture fashion, news, book publishing, art, political governance, and finance. This also includes advanced public services such as specialized hospitals, universities, and courts of law.

If you are thinking of the economic development of your city, you should make sure that these industries are doing well. They will not have a natural tendency to move out of the city. But if they dwindle, your city will suffer. Since you are a second-rank city, it will be difficult to hold on to a stock exchange, or the nation's political institutions. This is where you need to keep an eye on the dynamism of these industries.

An example of this is the fashion industry in Montreal. Yes, you read correctly. Montreal had a bustling fashion industry. It was made of a mix of Italian, Jewish, French-Canadian, and Portuguese entrepreneurs, suppliers of furs, leathers and textiles, seamstresses and designers, who produced all sorts of garments in what is now downtown. The industry was forced out by higher land values, and moved north, to the Chabanel district. Today, the industry is mostly gone, as most of our garments are made abroad.

I am not advocating for protecting industries from the necessary changes of a market economy. Higher land prices are part and parcel of a growing city. However, it is important for policy makers and analysts to understand the strong bonds that tie businesses together. You can't just move such an ecosystem to an industrial park without careful planning.

2. Transportation

Cities need to invest in their transportation infrastructure. It is the most productive investment a city can make. A maritime port which can unload ships faster, an airport that allows for more aircraft to land, highway infrastructure which increases connections with the most inventive and dynamic cities on the continent, improved railroads that connect the city with supply and transplant regions. All of these infrastructures are trade routes. When you invest in the scale, scope, and efficiency of trade routes, you are simultaneously reducing transport costs to your city, and from your city, which allows it to grow.

Theoretically, any improvement in transportation will be good for the city. However, given the massive issue of climate change, city development should focus on climate-friendly transportation, which will translate into more walking, cycling and transit for individual intracity movements, and more rail, and electrified engines for inter-city trade.

The ultimate proof of this, for me, is the modern economic history of Paris, France. When the decision was made for all railroads in France to converge on Paris, in the 19th century, the fate of cities not Paris was sealed for the next century and more. The development of Paris was immediate, rapid, and massive. It's as if the whole country moved to the capital city. It was so swift that the pressure on the water system was incredibly strong. Even in the 20th century, most city-dwellers in the eastern boroughs (arrondissements) did not have a bath, or a toilet. Granted, these populations came from poor rural locations, and France had been late in adopting modern industry and capitalism. But, to this day, the development of cities like Toulouse, Marseilles, and Lyon, has been directly affected by the centralization of rail transportation in France to the benefit of Paris.

About transit, one must be conscious of the importance of modes of transportation actually working together. You wouldn't build a subway system that people can't walk to, or cycle to. You want the railroad cars to transfer easily onto trucks and ships. You want the airport to be easily accessible by car, bus, and subway.

I would like to mention here that Montreal is not a class leader in this regard. We do enjoy a very efficient subway system, the métro. And given the density of the city in the urban residential areas, transit ridership is much higher in Montreal than in any other city in Canada.

However, one major mistake in the city's infrastructure, was to allow professional hockey interests to dislocate railroads in the downtown, to the benefit of the arena known as the Bell Centre, which houses the Montreal Canadiens NHL hockey club. Coming from the west, the Canadian Pacific railway now ends at the Lucien-L'Allier metro station, on one side of the arena. On the other side of the arena, you find an underground rail station used for the suburban rail service (Windsor Station), which goes north towards residential areas. A few hundred meters east, you also find the inter-city central train station (Gare centrales), connecting to the Canadian National Railway, offering destinations such as Ottawa, Toronto, New York City, Boston, Quebec City and Halifax. Because of a lack of vision in planning, the city allowed the arena to be built in such a way that none of these railways could connect to each other. The arena was built with a massive parking garage for automobiles, a few meters from the highway ramp.

The problem is the lack of interconnectivity between modes of transportation. As Jacobs points out, you can't really guess where people are going to go. But if they have options, they will probably use them. In the present configuration, we've reduced the number of options for people to conveniently travel in different directions. The less travelling, the less economic activity.

Today, Montreal is again given the opportunity to make a huge mistake in its transit investments. At the time of writing this, a very important transit project was still being redrawn: the REM de l'Est, a commuter rail line that would improve transit to the east end of the city. Hopefully, the decisions made by Quebec and the city in the remainder of 2022 will improve the connectivity of the proposed rail line.

Rather than planning and building new rail lines in conjunction with the existing underground subway (métro), the existing commuter trains (trains de banlieue), and the existing bus systems (STM and other transit authorities), the powers that be have delegated the new investments to Quebec's pension investment firm, the Caisse de dépôt et placement du Québec (not to be confused with the credit unions famously called Caisses populaires). The new commuter line, which improves access to underserved suburban areas, is called the REM (Réseau Express Métropolitain). The REM is a parallel service whose financial success depends on its independence from other rails and services. This will be true downtown, as first generation REM stations will not connect easily with métro stations. We should also note that the first generation

REM was supposed to connect downtown with the Montreal-Trudeau International Airport, but due to the COVID-19 pandemic, the airport has been unable to pay for its share of the project. Montreal is one of the world's most advanced cities yet to have a transit link to its main airport.

It may also be true in the newer investments in the east end of Montreal, where the REM authorities (at the time of publishing this text) refused to build a station connecting with the métro. The CDPQ has said the project will be more lucrative if the rails are separate, than if riders can switch from one train to the other. However, for the city, and its development, this is unfortunate. As Jacobs explained in her first book on urban planning, connecting modes of transportation provides new opportunities for development, increases the possible destinations, increases travelling traffic and would ultimately increase land values.

At the time of publication, the province yanked the east-end project from the CDPQ and had yet to publish a revised itinerary. We can only hope for improved connectivity with all other modes of transportation in the new proposal.

3. Education

Every city needs to invest in education. However, if your city is not the country's economic capital, it might want to double-down on technical and university education.

There are two axes to this argument. The first is to attract young talent to your city with strong institutions. These young people will require professors and other university employees, which is good for your city's cultural development, its real estate market, and general income pool. Young talent will grow your city's labour pool and maybe even become entrepreneurs. If they can't find work in the city, they won't be a burden because they can always go work in the capital or maybe even their hometown.

The second axis is to help your local industry develop and innovate. Universities must be considered through all of their functions. They provide cultural training for future filmmakers and video-game editors. They provide technical training for future engineers, doctors and computer programmers. They also provide scientific research for organizations and corporations who desperately need to stay ahead of their competition. All of these types of knowledge spillovers are important for the general economic development of the city.

4. Breakaway Entrepreneurs

Cities need to nurture their entrepreneurs. And second-rank cities need to do this even more so than their first-rank counterparts. There is a long list of innovation support policies that already exist, and this is certainly not the first time one has heard of the importance of this. Like most policy makers and analysts, I fully support the development of start-up accelerators, venture-capital funds, and business contests. I would however point to a phenomenon Jacobs wrote about abundantly which is the importance of the breakaway entrepreneur.

As of the mid-1990s, the image of the entrepreneur changed almost overnight. Previously, a middle-aged man from the trades or industry, the archetype of the entrepreneur was now touted as a teenaged computer-geek turned millionaire. Silicon Valley start-ups were founded by barely-adult coding whizzes. I think that as the techno-revolution eases, we may have lost sight of who needs the most encouragement to become an entrepreneur.

I encourage policy makers to think about encouraging middle-aged adults, in their forties or fifties, to break away from comfortable jobs and start a business in the field that they have the most experience. Breakaway entrepreneurship helps to bridge gaps in supply, it helps to diversify the corporate makeup of the city and allows for constant renewal of the economy.

5. Megas, solutions, and transplants

This section is for the industrial development agents. If you are working for a second-tier city, your city is probably not creating too many problems. Which means, it probably does not suffer from acute traffic, pollution, crime, or other urban ills. You would probably be tempted to use this as a selling point to attract business away from larger, more congested cities. This is a tricky strategy. The large corporations who have plants and offices they could move will probably play you against your competition. You have probably already been on the losing end of such negotiations. The reason is simple, you are not "the only game in town."

However, if you move quickly and keenly, you can identify foreign corporations who need an urban environment to thrive, but also need to move to your country to grow their business. Being a large city, you have more to offer in terms of economies of agglomeration than in terms of lower costs of production. This being said, your second-rank city is most probably more affordable to move to than the first-rank city in your country. Benefitting from both economies of agglomeration and slightly lower land costs, you have an argument. Look to large firms, in very, very large cities, in foreign countries. They may take a chance and open offices in your metropolis.

Quebec Separation and its Currency

Most second-rank cities will never have their own currency, which severely undermines their economic growth and development. I don't see a future, politically, where Boston would have a currency other than the US dollar. But if you ask Oslo, Norway, if it were to go back to being part of Sweden, and use its currency, the Swedish crown, the city would probably say no thank you.

Montreal's situation is a lot like Oslo, argued Jane Jacobs. If Quebec were to separate from Canada, it would have to decide on a currency. The issue of a currency in a sovereign Quebec is a hot potato. The Parti Québécois is notorious for advocating secession, without changing currencies, given the incredible change a new currency brings to everyone's daily life. However, most observers would agree that it would be inevitable for a separate Quebec to have its own currency. Jacobs actually wrote a book on this topic in 1980, where she addresses the many issues of Quebec secession, including the currency. Jacobs argued that were Quebec to become independent from Canada, it should start its own currency in planned stages, rather than stay with the Canadian dollar.

In Canada, all citizens and corporations must pay their taxes to the federal government, the issuer of the national currency, in Canadian dollars. This, with the usual provisions of legal tender are the only regulations that impose the use of the Canadian dollar in the economy. It is not illegal to start another currency in Canada, but you won't be able to use it to pay your taxes, or to clear debts in front of a judge. Given the multitude of taxes to pay, such as consumer taxes, gas taxes, income taxes and corporate taxes, this is enough to hinder the existence of any other currency.

The main economic argument that federalists invoke to stem support for Quebec's independence is that the new state would lose its share of "equalization" payments, a revenue-sharing scheme that allows poorer provinces to afford the same level of public spending as rich provinces. In Canada, the rich provinces are the oil-producers of Alberta, Saskatchewan, and Newfoundland, as well as Ontario, where you find the economic capital of the country. Quebec receives billions in equalization, and some see it as an off-set, or a compensation, for having to live with an exchange rate which does not float in the favour of the have-not provinces, including the only French-speaking province in the country.[2]

The questions related to currency, trade flows, and capital flows, are difficult to model in advance of an actual creation of a new currency. It is rife with uncertainty. For example, the monetary union which is Canada makes it impossible to measure a province's balance of inter-provincial payments, let alone its international payments. We've had ongoing debates in Quebec about the constant loss of headquarters to other parts of the world, but mostly to Toronto.

Sometimes, large transactions benefit Quebec, such as when aircraft and train maker Bombardier acquired Adtranz from Germany, or when the corner-store multinational Couche-Tard acquired Circle K from the USA. Other times, Quebec loses out, such as when the hardware chain Rona was acquired by Lowe's, an American giant, or when Bombardier, faced with the incapacity of competing with subsidized military contractors like Boeing, sold off assets to concentrate its efforts on private jets. Every time these transactions come up, questions arise about whether capital flows into Quebec are equivalent to capital flows out of the province. There is no way to measure this precisely. The reason is that banks in Canada are federally regulated (charter banks), and that bank accounts are not tallied per province, or city. It is therefore impossible to estimate Montreal's or Quebec's balance of international payments.

It might well be that the balance is negative, but without a methodology for obtaining the data, we don't know. If foreign capital tends to concentrate in oil-rich provinces, and in Toronto, where the stock market is located, and around which corporate headquarters agglomerate, then Quebec's capital flows just might be negative, given that our trade account (current account) is generally positive. Quebec is rich in resources, such as aluminum, hydroelectricity, gold, copper, and also exports goods such as aircraft, trucks, grains, and pork. Quebec is a big exporter.

This brings in foreign currency, which usually allows Quebec corporations to invest abroad. Economic theory posits that if your trade account is positive (Exports being more important than Imports), then your capital account (Foreign Investments in vs Investments out) needs to be negative, so that the sum of the international payments balance out. It is possible to have an imbalance of international payments, either positive or negative, but it is difficult to sustain for long periods. Usually, a floating exchange rate allows capital markets to realign themselves so that international payments are in balance. Obviously, Quebec does not have its own exchange rate, so that an imbalance could be sustained long-term.

Jacobs makes an important point in her 1980 book on Quebec secession. She writes that there is not really an economic rationale for Quebec to secede if it keeps the Canadian dollar. It would lose the equalization payments, suffer a certain amount of capital flight due to the predictable, and maybe even understandable, emotional reaction from English Canada, and not have the benefit of a floating exchange rate. However, she did predict that Montreal could not continue to be the top city in Canada if Quebec opted to stay in the country. Montreal would become a regional capital for French-speaking Canadians and basically subordinate to Toronto. It would be hard to argue that this is not the case today, more than 40 years after she made the prediction.

Jacobs proposed a measured solution. Given that Quebecers were weary of seceding, and that the idea of a new currency was not widely accepted, she proposed that the changes be made in phases, gradually. The first step would be to create a central bank, and later to print Quebec dollars at par with the Canadian dollar. The change is purely symbolic but allows people to become accustomed to the idea and allows the central bank time to develop its capacities. This is the case in Scotland, which collects the Seignorage fees on the fresh bills, so that the central bank is of no cost to taxpayers. Once the political and economic arrangements are finalized, which could take anywhere from two to 10 years, then the banking charters would be transferred to the new Quebec state. This critical step would allow the central bank to measure the actual balance of international payments, and then could decide, using hard data, to float the Quebec currency or not. Most observers believe the currency would slide, and my guess is it might be worth 75 percent of the Canadian dollar, or 60-70 cents to the US dollar.

The important thing to keep in mind is not that this would give Quebec an advantage on export markets (which it would), but that the currency would float, and this information would feed energy (work and capital) to the cities of Quebec, (mostly to Montreal), and allow for sustained economic growth. Given the incredible sense of curiosity and creativeness of Quebecers, I would not be surprised if, given some time, the currency would become more valuable than the Euro, the US dollar, or even the Pound. But that's not the important thing. The main issue is feedback, energy, and growth.

There is an important issue that needs to be addressed, which is the debts contracted by the Quebec government in Canadian dollars over the past decades. These bonds have to be honored in Canadian funds. However, the Quebec government would be collecting revenues in Quebec currency. If the said currency is devalued, it would make the bond payments much more expensive, which would be an important weight on the new country's finances. Of course, Quebec owns enough assets to cover these bonds, especially through the important public pension fund Caisse de dépôt et placement du Québec, and the public energy utility Hydro-Québec. Given the importance of Quebec financial institutions such as the cooperative Desjardins Movement and the Banque Nationale, capital flight is probably not as big an issue today as it was in 1980. Hopefully, the decision to float the currency would take into account the government's ability to honor past bonds, and to issue new bonds using the new currency.

I would also like to add that Quebec, and other parts of Canada, could have separate currencies without secession. This would need an important overhaul of the federal state apparatus. It would give much more fiscal powers to the province. And it is probably too much to ask of our politicians. In my view, this would probably put a definitive end to discussions about secession.

One last thing. There was a time in Canada when there were several currencies, even within the same city. In Montreal, each bank would print its own currency until 1934, when the Bank of Canada was created. The currencies were issued on the gold standard, and circulated on multiple notation systems such as the *piastre*, the *écu*, the penny, and the dollar. Evidence of this is available at the Museum of the Bank of Canada, which you can search online for pictures of bills and coins.

It was a free banking system. There were French-Canadian banks, such as the Banque du Peuple, the Banque de Saint-Laurent, and the Banque de Saint-Hyacinthe. There were also English-Canadian banks such as the Molson Bank and Henry's Bank. There might have been an exchange rate between cities, but I've never been able to find evidence of that.

In the United States, the 12 central banks which make up the Fed are evidence of the regional differences in the country's economy. When the federal government unified the currency system in 1863, and later created the Federal Reserve Bank in 1907, it gave up on regional exchange rates within the country.

History has a way of showing us that the world we live in is not always the only possibility.

Conclusion

The past few years have been difficult. The COVID-19 pandemic has forced many people to reorganize their lives in ways they had never imagined would have been necessary or even feasible. Couples have separated. Families have moved out of the core neighborhoods. Older folks are wintering in the country, rather than down south. Younger folks are buying vans, instead of backpacks and airline tickets. Lots of people are going back to school, only to find it difficult to concentrate in online classes. Many small business owners have lost their sources of income. Government-imposed lockdowns slowed traffic in our cities. Rebates on gas prices, in the spring of 2019, are difficult to recall. Gasoline was inexpensive, but no one had anywhere to go. Office towers emptied out. Downtown streets went empty. Demand for country living increased. Large homes with space for a home office became the norm. Restaurants, clubs, and bars were shut down, discouraging commuters from visiting the inner city at all.

So, do cities still matter?

It's a good question.

There are lots of people who actually don't like cities. Maybe it's due to social anxiety. Some people don't feel comfortable in crowds, in the underground trains, in buses, in traffic, in an office building. Maybe it's due to convenience. Many office workers got used to working from home, benefiting from homemade meals, and saving time on commutes. Who wants to spend an hour each way on a bus or a train? Working parents got a huge break during the pandemic, having more time to play with their children, to bake bread, and to slow down their hectic schedules.

But there are lots of people who love cities. They love the clubs, the bars, the restaurants, the health gyms, and spas. They love the excitement of the city. There is life here. They love working in shared office spaces. Personally, previously as a journalist, and now as a teacher, I really like having colleagues hanging around the office. These are people who share so much with me, their ideas, their successes, their challenges. We are better teachers, writers, and colleagues for having neighbors to interact with.

In the summer of 2020, a dispute arose in New York City between a comedy club owner and the famous comedian Jerry Seinfeld. The former argued the city was doomed. Covid was killing New York City. Of course, his club was closed and the level of activity in the city had slowed to a halt. But Seinfeld argued that the city would recover. It was not going to be easy, but just as cities have recovered from pandemics in the past, so too would New York City recover from the coronavirus. The debate went viral and forced economists to get in touch with their inner Jacobs. Jeffrey Sachs, a professor of sustainable development at Columbia University, chimed in. Sachs believes that cities will come through for three reasons. First, Covid won't last forever and the city will learn how to better cope and prepare. Sachs adds that lower rent prices will help cities repurpose themselves. Jacobs also wrote that in 1969. Second, cities are more productive than rural areas, except for farms. Third, people like cities.

Of course, I think Sachs is right. He is basically recanting Jacobs' views, that cities solve problems better than other modes of human organisation. The question is really about the future of humanity. Sachs ends his opinion piece with a warning about social inequality. Cities are liked by many, including the ultra-rich. The income divide has worsened during the pandemic. Owners of online services such as Amazon and Netflix have thrived. I agree with Sachs that this is a dangerous social experiment. Hopefully, social equity is something that cities can solve. Most social justice movements have been quite urban, such as the labour movements, feminist movements, and civil rights movements of the past century.

The question we must tackle is what kind of society do we want to live in? Do we want to tackle the issue of climate change? Do we want to tackle social justice? Do we want peace in the world?

If we want solutions, we need healthy cities. Cities matter because they find solutions to our problems, the problems that we, as humans, have created.

In her last book *Dark Age Ahead*, Jacobs warned us of many social ills that would hinder the continued development of Euro-American society (or empire). For each of these ills, cities can be part of the solution. A major issue for her was the fact that in the 1990s and 2000s, families became rigged to fail. House prices have inflated so much that families can no longer afford the middle-class lifestyle of their parents. Since the end of the 2010s, things have only gotten worse. Families seeking affordable housing have fled to lower-density cities and suburbs. But this is not going to be of much help later on, when gas prices increase on the need to reduce greenhouse gases and to revert climate change. Affordable housing for families in urban environments is the only possible solution to solve both the issue of a family's quality of living, and of the climate.

Cities also matter because they are the best way for us to organize invention and innovation. An aspect of the last few years that concerns me is the shift our labour market has taken towards a standardization of many tasks. As people work from home, meetings take place on video-conferencing software, such as Zoom or Teams. These actually tend to be time consuming, as internet lags, buffering between speakers, and human-nature itself make meetings less productive. Worker supervision is difficult. I wonder how companies can continue to operate smoothly if the higher-up c-suite executives are concerned with the efficiency of their management structure. Who knows what employee n. 12345 is actually doing right now? Who knows if employee n. 12345 actually exists?

Many workers argue they are more productive than ever. That may be. But I am thinking about the standardization of work. If management is concerned with supply concerns, organizations will tend to focus on doing what's most pressing, and forego decisions on future projects, on new products, on innovative services.

Who can innovate when, in the middle of a pandemic, an organization needs to concentrate on saving its core business? Who can innovate when people don't want to meet, won't even shake hands to seal the deal? How can you trust someone with a risky project if you won't even trust him enough to shake his hand?

What cities are good at is producing services where tacit information, rather than standardized information, is most important. For example, if a store orders white athletic socks, it doesn't really matter where they are produced because the product is so standardized, so mature, so predictable, that the only question purchasers have on their minds is the price. However, if a store orders fashion socks, it does matter where they are produced because they might have to change colours at the last minute.

What was cool last week might be worth nothing more than a rag the next. This is where the local fashion industry has an advantage over the delocalized plant. This example is not unique to fashion. It applies to most industries. When a corporation decides to change strategies, accounting and legal firms need to be close by to advise and rewrite paperwork. When a restaurant decides to change its menu, food suppliers must be available to discuss the availability of ingredients. When schools decide to start a new music program, students need to be willing to commute to school to practice their instruments. When things change, when specifications need to be re-designed, when trends move fast, then the human factor needs to be closely bonded.

Organizations tend to fail when they can't adapt themselves to the changing times. This is why Kodak and Research in Motion have basically disappeared. This is also why IBM spends so much time and energy on innovation. What used to be cutting-edge International Business Machines, could very well have failed many times in the face of competition from Apple, Google, Microsoft, or Amazon.

Cities are the research and development laboratory for humanity. Cities are where people interact, where they create bonds, and build relationships. This is why they matter, and they won't go away. Humanity still has many problems to fix, and they need healthy cities to get through it all.

Notes

Chapter 1 - Economies of Agglomeration
1. This figure comes from my own research, which covered the geography of patents in Quebec from 1972-1993. Université de Sherbrooke, Master's thesis, 2004.

Chapter 3 - Urban Land Values
1. In Montreal, these neighborhoods are Westmount and Outremont.

Section 2 – Jacobs' Urban Economics
1. References to economists who have studied Jacobs hypotheses are listed in "Jane Jacobs Among the Economists," by David Nowlan, published as a chapter from Max Allen (ed), *Ideas That Matter: The Worlds of Jane Jacobs*, The Ginger Press, 1997, pp. 111-113.

Chapter 4 – Jacobs' Theory of Import Replacement
1. This concept is similar, but different, from the strategy of import-substitution, which usually is applied on large-scale projects, such as energy supply, or large manufacturing facilities. Import-substitution fell out of fashion as an economic development strategy with the advent of globalization. Import-substitution is often based on governmental trade barriers such as tariffs, and subsidies, whereas Jacobs' idea of Import-replacement is based on open trade, and small-scale breakaway entrepreneurship.

2. This principle should be widely accepted by economists, as it is a basic assumption in microeconomic theory, specifically when discussing indifference curves.

3. An overview of empirical work in the literature can be found in Essletzbichler (2007). In Quebec, a high industrial diversity at the regional (MRC) level has been associated with steady and strong economic growth, whereas low industrial diversity is associated to low wealth, and/or wild variations in growth (Trempe, 2006).

Chapter 6 – Cities and Nation-States

1. If you would like to learn more about Jacobs' thinking behind this idea of largesse, I recommend her 1994 book called *Systems of Survival*. It explains how governments are usually animated by a desire to act as guardians of the land, which predisposes them to distribute funds as *largesse* across the land, as opposed to businesspeople who are animated by a desire to trade, and who focus on the mutual benefits of transactions.

2. Nowadays, a city currency in Montreal would probably be priced lower than the Canadian dollar. It would help Montreal sell exports and bolster its economy. A regional currency in the West would still be strong, with no negative impact on the Alberta resource economy.

Chapter 7 - The Forward City

1. Jacobs never used the terms Jacobs' Agglomeration, or Forward City. She used the term "import-replacing city."

2. See Mazzucato (2002)

Chapter 10 - The Supply Region

1. In Canada, the federal government transfers equalization payments to poor provinces, which are generated from taxes collected in wealthy provinces such as Alberta (wealthy supply region), or Ontario (Toronto is a wealthy forward city).

2. For example, Alberta's oil patch dictates fluctuations in the Canadian exchange rate. However, the oil industry cycle may not match the cycle for shipbuilding, which is a major export work for Nova Scotia. Hence, the monetary union of the Canadian dollar may be hurting the Maritime economy more than it helps.

Chapter 13 - Innovation in Jacobs' Agglomerations

1. The "ideas in imports" concept seems to be slowly gaining traction in academic fields. In a recent study on OECD countries, Bournakis, Christopoulos and Mallick (2018) measured the spillovers associated with international trade. They concluded that "international knowledge spillover is an important driver of industry output per worker, and the magnitude of this spillover effect varies with alternative assumptions about the information content embodied in imports, while high technology industries benefit significantly more from import-related knowledge spillovers." Unfortunately, the authors do not cite Jacobs as being the original seminal author of this concept. Her contribution, written in 1969, thus goes largely ignored in the field of economics.

Chapter 14 - Diversity Trumps Specialization

1. The study of industrial clusters had a golden age in the 1990s and 2000s, under the leadership of economists such as Michael Porter, Edward Glaeser, and Richard Florida. It is not obvious to me that the economies of agglomeration associated with innovation clusters are any different than in regular cities. What I mean by that is that aerospace companies don't necessarily need to be co-located in the same district. They tend to benefit from the externalities of the cluster by being in the same large metropolitan agglomeration. I leave it to empirical researchers to hash out the details of that question. See Bathelt, Feldman, & Kogler (2014).

2. The latter proposition is hard to demonstrate empirically, mostly because of a lack of data. Many studies have used patent data to measure spillovers, but many innovations are never patented, which makes it hard to track the influences of a large unquantifiable share of innovation. Spillovers rely on ad hoc phenomena which are profoundly human in nature. If you are looking for a linear cause-effect relationship, you may not find it here. See Desrochers (1998).

Chapter 15 - The Future of Montreal and 2nd-rank cities

1. I am tempted to add most of the European capitals in this list as they are subject to financial energies being concentrated in Frankfurt, Germany. Most of the southern regions of Europe

are now dependent on transfers from the European Union, such as southern Italy, much of Spain, much of Portugal, and almost the entirety of Greece. Even Paris is struggling to grow since it has forsaken the Franc to join the Eurozone. This same analysis applies to all large monetary unions, such as the US, India, and China.

2. Coulombe has proposed that the equalization payments are insufficient to cover the losses in manufacturing jobs, caused by Dutch Disease in Canada, a trade concept that implies that resource endowments can inflate the national currency's value on foreign markets, which will undermine domestic economic development and manufacturing sectors.

Notes on Sources – References and Further Reading

CHAPTER 1
Glaeser, E. L. (Editor). (2010). *Agglomeration Economics*. Chicago : University of Chicago Press.

Jacobs, J. (1969). *The Economy of Cities*. Vintage.

Marshall, A. (1920). *Principles of Economics*. London: MacMillan.

CHAPTER 2
Polèse, M., Shearmur, R. & Terral, L. (2015). *Économie Urbaine et Régionale: Géographie Économique 4ᵉ Éd*. Economica.

CHAPTER 4
Caragliu, A., de Dominicis, L., & de Groot, H. L. F. (2016). "Both Marshall and Jacobs were Right!" *Economic Geography*. Vol. 92 Issue 1, p87-111.

Desrochers, P. & Hospers, G.-J. (2007). "Cities and the economic development of nations: An essay on Jane Jacobs' contribution to economic theory." *Canadian Journal of Regional Science*. (Spring 2007), 115-130.

Essletzbichler, J. (2007). "Diversity, stability and regional growth in the U.S. (1975-2002)." In Frenken, K. (Ed.) *Applied Evolutionary Economics and Economic Geography*. London: Edward Elgar Publishing.

Ikeda, S. (2011). "Economic Development from a Jacobsian Perspective. Presented at Colloquium on Market Institutions and Economic Processes," New York University, 28 February 2011.

Jacobs, J. (1969). *The Economy of Cities*. Vintage.

Jacobs, J. (2011). *The Question of Separatism, Quebec and the Struggle over Sovereignty*. Baraka Books. Originally published in 1980 by Random House.

Jacobs, J. (1985). *Cities and the Wealth of Nations*, Principles of Economic Life. Vintage.

Nowlan, D. M. (1997). "Jane Jacobs Among the Economists." Published in Max Allen (ed), *Ideas That Matter: The Worlds of Jane Jacobs*, The Ginger Press, 1997, pp. 111-113.

Trempe, P. (2006). *Diversité industrielle et Développement économiques selon les MRC en 2001*. Québec: Ministère du développement économique, de l'innovation et de l'exportation.

CHAPTER 5

Jacobs, J. (1985). *Cities and the Wealth of Nations, Principles of Economic Life*. Vintage.

Schumpeter, A. (1942). *Capitalism, Socialism, and Democracy*. Harper and Brothers.

CHAPTER 6

Jacobs, J. (1969). *The Economy of Cities*. Vintage.

Jacobs, J. (1985). *Cities and the Wealth of Nations*. Vintage.

Jacobs, J. (1994). *Systems of Survival, A Dialogue on the Moral Foundations of Commerce and Politics*. Vintage.

CHAPTER 12

Jacobs, J. (1969). *The Economy of Cities*. Vintage.

Jacobs, J. (1985). *Cities and the Wealth of Nations*. Vintage.

Mazzucato, M. (2002). "The PC Industry: New Economy or Early Life-Cycle," *Review of Economic Dynamics*, Vol. 5 (2), pp. 318–345.

CHAPTER 14

Bathelt, H., Feldman, M. & Kogler, D. F. (Editors). (2013). *Beyond Territory. Dynamic Geographies of Knowledge Creation, Diffusion, and Innovation*. Routledge.

Bournakis, I., Christopoulos, D. & Mallick, S. (2018). "Knowledge Spillovers and Output Per Worker: An Industry-Level Analysis For OECD Countries." *Economic Inquiry*. 56 (2).

Bureau of Economic Analysis. https://www.bea.gov/help/faq/478

Desrochers, P. (1998). "On the Abuse of Patents as Economic Indicators." *The Quarterly Journal of Austrian Economics*. 1 (4).

Hall, P. (1966) *The World Cities*. McGraw-Hill.

Jacobs, J. (1969). *The Economy of Cities*. Vintage.

Jacobs, J. (1984). *Cities and the Wealth of Nations*. Vintage.

Trempe, P. (2006). *Diversité industrielle et Développement économiques selon les MRC en 2001*. Québec: Ministère du Développement économique, de l'innovation et de l'exportation.

CHAPTER 15

Coulombe, S. (2014). "Le mal hollandais, le fédéralisme fiscal et l'économie du Québec" dans *Le Québec économique - Volume 5: Les grands enjeux de finances publiques*. Luc Godbout et Marcelin Joanis (ed.), Presses de l'Université Laval, chapitre 7.

Dauphin, R. (1994). *L'Economie du Québec, une économie à la remorque de ses groupes*. Beauchemin Éditeur.

Jacobs, J. (1969). *The Economy of Cities*. Vintage.

Jacobs, J. (2011). *The Question of Separatism, Quebec and the Struggle over Sovereignty*. Baraka Books. Originally published in 1980 by Random House.

Jacobs, J. (1985). *Cities and the Wealth of Nations*. Vintage.

Jacobs, J. (1994). *Systems of Survival, A Dialogue on the Moral Foundations of Commerce and Politics*. Vintage.

Rudin, R. (1985). *Banking en français: The French Banks of Quebec 1835-1925*. University of Toronto Press.

CONCLUSION

Sachs, J. D. (2020). Jerry Seinfeld is right about New York's future. CNN.COM. https://www.cnn.com/2020/08/27/opinions/jerry-seinfeld-right-about-new-york-sachs/index.html

Printed by Imprimerie Gauvin
Gatineau, Québec